CALLED TO LOVE

CALLED TO LOVE

· · · ·

Approaching John Paul II's Theology of the Body

CARL ANDERSON

AND

JOSÉ GRANADOS

IMAGE
NEW YORK

All right reserved.
Published in the United States by Image, an imprint
of The Crown Publishing Group, a division of
Random House, Inc., New York.
www.crownpublishing.com

IMAGE is a registered trademark, and the "I" colophon is a
trademark of Random House, Inc.

Originally published in hardcover in the United States
by Doubleday Religion, New York, in 2009.

Library of Congress Cataloging-in-Publication Data
Anderson, Carl.
Called to love: approaching John Paul II's theology of the body / Carl
Anderson and José Granados.
p. cm.
Includes bibliographical references.
1. John Paul II, Pope, 1920–2005. Theology of the body. 2. Body,
Human—Religious aspects—Catholic Church. 3. Catholic Church—
Doctrines. I. Granados, José. II. Title.
BX1795.B63A53 2009
233'.5—dc22
2008042909

ISBN 978-0-7704-3574-5
E-ISBN 978-0-385-52958-7

Book design by Lovedog Studios

First Paperback Edition

147905709

CONTENTS

PREFACE

For you formed my inward parts, you knitted me together in my mother's womb.

I praise you, for you are fearful and wonderful.

Wonderful are your works! You know me right well. (Ps. 139)

The Psalmist's wonder before his own body leads him to praise his Creator, who makes himself and his provident care and intimate knowledge of us perceptible precisely in the body. This is the "prophetism of the body," as John Paul II used to say. The body speaks of God; it reveals his goodness and wisdom. It also speaks of us, of man and woman and our vocation to love. This is a prophetic word, pronounced by the body in God's name, revealing to us the path to take toward human fulfillment: the way of love, in which the original image imprinted in man and woman can be realized and shine forth in a fruitful communion of persons, open to the gift of life.

We are coming out of centuries in which, due to the influence of a dualistic mentality colored by Manichaeism and Puritanism, the human body has been despised or at least insufficiently valued. It was viewed with suspicion and apprehension, as if it were a threat to man's spiritual nature and destiny. It was neglected or denied in its affective and sexual dimension, as though it were unavoidably fraught with temptations and dangers. Today, the pendulum seems to have swung to the opposite extreme with the worship of the body, exalting it so long as it is young, beautiful, and pleasurable, but then rejecting it when it testifies to its inevitable decline, illness, and death. Beyond the apparent contradiction, in reality these two positions share the same anthropological reductionism that is unable to integrate the body into the reality of the person and hence incapable of adequately appreciating the body's subjectivity. The body thus ends up losing its mystery and is made a banality.

Among the greatest gifts John Paul II has bequeathed to the Church and humanity is surely his "theology of the body," which has enabled us to rediscover the full treasure of biblical anthropology and the great Christian tradition, thereby overcoming narrow and marginal perspectives, and to integrate it into a vision consonant with lived experience grasped with new vividness.

For a right appreciation of the body, it is necessary to cultivate a contemplative gaze, one that grasps the body's mystery in relation to the person and the vocation to love, which is definitively illuminated and fulfilled in the Risen Christ. Hence the importance of this volume: much more than a superficial show of enthusiasm for the novelty of the theology of the body, it sheds light on its anthropological foundations with a language at once simple, poetic, and profound.

The authors of this work have succeeded in presenting the content of John Paul II's Great Catechesis on human love in the divine plan, given from 1979 to 1984, in such a way as to make it accessible without watering it down. Their contribution has certain characteristic qualities that make it original and invaluable:

1. The presentation of the essential elements of the "theology of the body" with the help of Karol Wotyla's poetry and texts from great works of the literary, poetic, and philosophical tradition makes for evocative reading that invites comparison with the reader's own experiences.

2. The insertion of John Paul II's "theology of the body" in the context of Benedict XVI's "theology of love" widens the theological horizons of the anthropological approach by founding it in a Christological and Trinitarian vision.

3. The underscoring of its social dimension: The theology of the body has in fact demonstrated how the communion of persons constitutes an authentic common good at the foundation of society and makes the civilization of love possible.

4. Its connection with the patristic and theological tradition of the Church is made clear by means of enlightening references. The novelty of the "theology of the body" is therefore put into historical perspective, without separation or opposition. In fact, the true newness of Christianity resides not in a break with tradition, but in the renewed freshness of the beginning, whose truth is continually demonstrated to arouse wonder and to provoke conversion and a more beautiful life.

I am certain that reading this accessible and precious book, the fruit of the reflection of two prestigious professors of the United States Session of the Pontifical John Paul II Institute for Studies on Marriage and Family, will contribute to showing the human beauty of the Christian proposal, which in the light of faith is able to make the love between a man and a woman shine with ever new light.

Livio Melina
President of the Pontifical John Paul II Institute
for Studies on Marriage and Family

ABBREVIATIONS

DCE: Deus Caritas Est

GS: Gaudium et Spes

JS: The Jeweler's Shop: A Meditation on the Sacrament of Matrimony Passing on Occasion into a Drama

LG: Lumen Gentium

LR: Love and Responsibility

MD: Mulieris Dignitatem (Letter to Women)

OGB: Our God's Brother

Ref Fath: Reflections on Fatherhood

RF: Radiation of Fatherhood

RH: Redemptor Hominis

RT: Roman Triptych

TOB: Man and Woman He Created Them: A Theology of the Body

MAN, THE WAY OF THE CHURCH— LOVE, THE WAY OF MAN

TOWARD THE END OF HIS LIFE, POPE JOHN PAUL II RE-turned to the art of poetry and left us a kind of literary testament, entitled *Roman Triptych*, which weaves together essential themes from both his experience and his thought. The first lines of the poem evoke a vision of nature: The pope describes how all of creation is in motion and everything strives to find its place, like "the stream's silvery cascade, rhythmically falling from the mountain, carried by its own current" (*RT*, 7). The poet even compares himself at one point to this flowing water, caught up in nature's rhythm and swept along by the tide of time. Nevertheless, he notes a crucial difference between a stream's descent down the mountainside and man's journey through life—a difference on which everything else we say in this book turns:

What do you say to me, mountain stream?
Where do you encounter me?
as I wend my own way—

just like you . . .
But really like you? (*RT*, 7)

QUESTIONING AND WONDER

So what sets man apart from the "silvery cascade"? The stream is borne along by its own weight, which carries it to the great river that eventually empties into the sea. But man is not content merely "to exist and follow his way" (*RT*, 8). On the contrary, man's existence is truly human only to the extent that he rises above the rhythm of the universe and cries: "Stop!" What distinguishes man from the rest of the visible creation is his propensity to step back from the cosmic dance and to ask about the meaning of it all: "What do you say to me?" (*RT*, 7).

Man's questioning is awakened by the spectacle of nature, but it does not stop there. The question man poses about the natural world spills over into a question about what lies in the depth of his own heart.[1] Man's question about nature is ultimately a question about *man himself*: "Where do you, world, encounter *me*?" (cf. *RT*, 7) What is the meaning of my own journey through life? The stream flows on without asking why, but every human being can identify with Saint Augustine's remark in the *Confessions*: "I became for myself a great question."[2]

John Paul II threw himself passionately into man's perennial question about the meaning of human life. The pope pursued the answer to this great question along the existential path of human experience. He was convinced that if we follow this path with the requisite insight, it will eventually lead us to the goal of our lives.[3]

As he put it in his first encyclical: "the way of man is the way of the Church" (*RH*, 1).

Admittedly, certain difficulties arise when we try to deal with the primordial question: What is man? Who am I? In the first place, we might wonder about the question itself: Is it really the first step on a journey toward the meaning of life, or is it just a riddle without an answer? Karol Wojtyla wrestled with this problem in the plays he wrote during his time as a pastor in Poland. Take *The Jeweler's Shop*, which Wojtyla published in 1960, two years after he was named a bishop. Here the future pope probes the meaning of married love as reflected in the stories of three different couples facing decisive turning points in their relationships. Wojtyla introduces us to the first couple, Teresa and Andrew, as the young pair ponder the meaning of their relationship, which is about to blossom into marriage. At a certain point, Teresa recalls a nighttime hike in the mountains she and Andrew had made with a group of friends years earlier. Teresa remembers being struck by the unsettling contrast between the harmony of nature and the disharmony within her own heart. Comparing the beauty of the world around her with her own interior uncertainty at that moment, Teresa exclaims, "Only man seems to be off balance and lost" (see *JS*, 29). In Wojtyla's *Radiation of Fatherhood*, Adam, who represents our common humanity, introduces himself by confessing a similar sense of alienation: "For many years I have lived like a man exiled from my deeper personality yet condemned to probe it" (*RF*, 335).

Because it isn't easy to find an answer to the question deep within us, we are tempted to narrow the question's scope. We try to force it into a tighter, supposedly more manageable form. We reduce man's search for his identity to a problem we believe can be solved by diligent application of the techniques of the natural sciences. John Paul II reacted vigorously against this reductionism, which, in the end, denies the soul's true depth and so leads to the abolition of man.

John Paul's rejection of reductionism is illustrated by the character of Adam Chmielowski, the protagonist of another play from his Polish period, *Our God's Brother*. At one point in the play, Adam, a gifted artist who has given up painting in order to help the poor, converses with a stranger who claims that an abundance of material goods is an adequate answer to the problem of poverty. Although Adam certainly does not discount man's material needs, he answers the stranger by pointing out the inexhaustibility of human desire: "Man's poverty is deeper than the resources of all those goods" (*OGB*, 242).

"Man's poverty is deeper than the resources of all those goods." Once we realize this truth and resist the allure of materialistic answers to the human question, another difficulty appears on the horizon: The very depth of the question can discourage us from searching for an answer. After all, isn't the answer too lofty for us? Doesn't it lie beyond the reach of our native capacity? Mightn't our search lead to unending debates that never quite manage to dispel our doubts?

John Paul II vigorously opposed this counsel of despair. Admittedly, the great question of human identity is in some sense bigger than the questioner. Nevertheless, the question is not the decisive thing (just as the capacity to question isn't the chief difference between man and the animals). On the contrary, *our questioning itself responds to something prior and more important*:

What do you say to me, mountain stream?
Where do you encounter me?

as I wend my own way—
just like you . . .
But really like you?
(Here let me pause;
let me halt before a threshold,
the threshold of pure wonder.)
The rushing stream cannot wonder,
as it descends, and the woods silently slope,
following its rhythm
—but man can wonder!
The threshold which the world crosses in him
is the threshold of wonder.
(Once this very wonder was given a name: "Adam.") (*RT*, 8)

Man's question about his own identity, the pope is telling us in this passage from *Roman Triptych*, does not arise in a vacuum, and therefore it is no mere enigmatic riddle with no answer. Rather man's questioning awakens in response to an experience of *wonder* that precedes it. Wonder gives birth to the question about who we are, and this priority of wonder determines the very nature of our search for an answer to it. Let's illustrate this point with an example from everyday life.

Suppose you're taking an exam and a question comes up that you didn't study for. Since this unexpected question catches you off guard, you experience it as a frustrating puzzle you can't solve. But let us imagine a different scenario. Say you receive an unexpected present from a friend. You may not know why he has given you this particular gift, but your question about what prompted this act of generosity is totally different, because you already know that the answer has to do with your friend's love for you. The gift moves you

to ask why, but the question does not paralyze you in the same way
an unexpected exam question would. Instead it opens up new paths
for, and possibilities of, friendship. The search for understanding is
meaningful at its very origin; indeed, the meaning is already there
long before the answer comes into view.

The question of man is more like the question prompted by a
friend's gift than it is like a puzzling problem on a math test, because
the question of man starts with wonder, which keeps the question
from degenerating into some enigma coming out of nowhere. Because wonder is not called forth by a lack of meaning but by an excess
of it, the questioning it provokes has nothing in common with an
abyss of sterile doubt that chokes off the stream of life—like Ham-
let's "to be or not to be?" Wonder assures us that there really is an
answer to the question. Of course, it also tells us that this answer is
not completely within our grasp. Yet this is actually a positive message, because when the answer does come, it will be even greater and
better than we could have imagined. Instead of paralyzing us, then,
wonder sustains us on our journey toward our true identity:

> Man went his way . . .
> carried along by wonder!
> In his wonderment, he always emerged
> from the tide that bore him on,
> as if to say to everything around him:
> "Stop! . . .
> all this passing has sense"
> "has sense . . . has sense . . . has sense!" (*RT*, 8)

At this point, we need to introduce a new term that captures that
special quality in things that makes them wonderful in our eyes. This

term is "mystery." Whereas in common parlance "mystery" means an obscurity that frustrates understanding, we'll be using the word in a much more positive sense that better reflects its original meaning. When we describe the world as "mysterious," our point is not that the world is inscrutable. Actually, we're saying just the opposite: The world is mysterious, not because it *lacks* meaning, but precisely because it is *saturated* with meaning. It's just that this meaning is too rich and full for the eyes of the mind to master in a single glance. Another way of putting this is that mystery is the calling card of reality; mystery is the ability to evoke wonder that is built into everything that really exists, no matter how seemingly trivial. In a word, mystery prompts us to question, not because there is a lack of clarity, but because there is an excess of light.

Man, Saint Augustine observed, is a great question for himself. Why? Because he is a great mystery that elicits wonder. Because man is a question that arises within wonder, he is not totally "off balance and lost" (*JS*, 29). He need not be discouraged in his search for an answer to the question that he himself is, because wonder gives him a "compass" for his journey toward fuller understanding. But where does man encounter the mystery that gives rise to his wonderment in the first place?

LOVE IS THE BIRTHPLACE OF WONDER

Many people today are in search of the mysterious, which they regard as a bulwark against enslavement to technology. More and more of our contemporaries glimpse that there is a mysterious depth to human existence, realize that it has been obscured, and are in the process of trying to recover it. But even if there is a growing consensus that mystery is the native atmosphere in which the question of meaning can breathe free, there is one issue that is still hotly debated: Where do we actually *encounter* this mystery?

A lot of people think that experiencing mystery means having some sort of mystical rapture apart from everyday existence. According to this mind-set, God cannot be found in the merely earthly but has to be sought exclusively in the depth of our souls. Unfortunately, this approach to mystery (which is fairly common in "New Age" circles) drives a wedge between religious experience and everyday existence. By the same logic, it reinforces the tendency to separate faith and life, which John Paul II identified as one of the biggest temptations facing modern man (see *Veritatis Splendor*, 26). The quest for mystery is a good thing, but not if it separates us from the world. For such a separation causes a rift in human existence; it turns us into mental schizophrenics who divide up our lives into supposedly airtight halves: on the one side, the concerns of the individual (religion and morality); on the other side, the supposedly universal concerns that make up the "real business" of our life in society (the realm of science and technology, politics and public policy, commerce and finance, and so on).

John Paul II offers a biblical contrast to this compartmentalization of man's identity. The habitat of wonder, he says, "is not in heaven, that you should say, 'Who will go up for us to heaven, and bring it to us, that we may hear it and do it?' Neither is it beyond the sea, that you should say, 'Who will go over the sea for us, and bring it to us, that we may hear it and do it?' " (Deut. 30:12–13)*. We meet wonder in the very midst of our everyday experience. We have already seen

---

* Note: Translations of the Bible are taken from the RSV, with occasional slight modifications when this was deemed necessary.

that man's contemplation of nature gives birth to wonder in his soul. But the amazement we experience at the sight of majestic mountains or of the immense ocean is not the first or most important kind of wonder. There is an even more basic experience of wonderment. The passage from *The Jeweler's Shop* we quoted previously suggests where the true birthplace of wonder lies.

The context, remember, is Teresa's recollection of the beauty of a certain night in the mountains. She contrasts this harmonious beauty to her earlier relationship with Andrew, who would eventually become her husband. Although the two were together on that nighttime hike through the mountains, the immaturity of Andrew's love for Teresa hindered their mutual understanding. Here is Teresa describing her feelings at the time:

> And I felt how difficult it is to live. That night was terribly hard
>   for me,
> though it was a truly glorious mountain night,
> and full of nature's secrets.
> Everything around seemed
> so very necessary
> and so in harmony with the world's totality,
> only man was off balance and lost. (*JS*, 29)

At the time Teresa re-creates for us in this soliloquy, she was incapable of welcoming reality in a spirit of wonderment; she had lost her way, and even a glorious mountain night could evoke only fear, disquiet, and confusion in her mind. Teresa's recollection underscores that man's unique ability to ask about the meaning of life is inseparable from his experience of love. Where love is missing, the question of meaning lacks the air it needs to catch fire. Later on,

when Andrew asks for Teresa's hand, this harmony of mutual understanding restores the balance she lacked on that nighttime hike.
It makes her receptive to the signal of love, which is even stronger
than the signals nature broadcasts to us through the silent majesty
of the mountains at night. In a word, the experience of love is the
birthplace of wonder, the first step along a new journey toward the
fullness of meaning.

If we had to choose a scene that captures the essence of wonder,
we might pick the moment when a child discovers the presents his
parents have laid under the Christmas tree for him. Or the face of
the mother who holds her newborn child in her arms for the very
first time. No matter which picture we choose, though, the point
is always the same: Wonder can be born only in the matrix of love.
Even the amazement that fills us when we behold the marvels of creation makes sense only in light of the experience of love, as we will
try to show in the following chapters of this book. Once again, the
experience of love is the birthplace of wonder.

John Paul's message to us, then, is that the source of wonder is not
far from our everyday experience, but that it reveals its presence in
the experience of love that accompanies every person from the cradle
to the grave. By the same token, our response to true love fulfills our
experience of wonder and puts in our hands a compass to guide our
quest for meaning to the goal of true happiness. "Man," John Paul II
writes in his first encyclical, "remains a being that is incomprehensible for himself, his life is senseless, if love is not revealed to him, if
he does not encounter love" (*RH*, 10).

Anna, another character in *The Jeweler's Shop*, receives a similar
revelation. Although Anna is a middle-aged woman in a troubled
marriage, what she learns about love applies to all of us: "Take you,
for instance. You cannot live without love. I saw from a distance how

you walked down the street and tried to rouse interest. I could almost hear your soul. You were calling with despair for a love you do not have. You were looking for someone who would take you by the hand and hug you" (*JS*, 64).

This passage captures the universal truth that love is the very substance of our lives and the revelation of our destiny. "Love," says Karol Wojtyla, "has the taste of the whole life of man. It has the weight of his whole existence. It cannot be a single moment" (*JS*, 60). The pope is right. Love does indeed touch all the dimensions of human life: It includes my body, my instincts, and my emotions, even as love flowers in a spiritual appreciation of the special dignity of the beloved and his or her connection with the transcendent Source of reality. By the same token, love is a guide that leads us beyond ourselves and toward transcendence. Love is thus the thread that reconnects the disjointed compartments into which modern man has divided up his life, and so restores the unity of which today's growing fragmentation increasingly robs us.

The experience of love is the foundation of John Paul II's vision of man. It is the key that enables him to address the human question from the inside and to take man's concerns and problems seriously. At the same time, John Paul's emphasis on love avoids the isolation and subjectivism into which our modern definition of experience often leads us. If *love* is the core of experience, then the latter can't be the purely individual and private affair we moderns tend to imagine. Love resonates in the depth of our soul, but it also takes us out of ourselves and ushers us into a fullness of life that is bigger than our tiny selves. The heart of experience, then, is the wonder awakened by the *revelation* of love. Love opens the very roots of the human person to the encounter with the other, to transcendence, and to newness of life.

HUMAN EXPERIENCE AND
DIVINE REVELATION

Let's go back for a moment to John Paul II's warning against separating faith and life. All too often Christians have reinforced this separation by treating their own religious experience as a foreign body alien to everyday life. Some critics of Christianity have mistaken this caricature for the real thing and have complained that the Christian religion destroys happiness and spoils the enjoyment of life by teaching man to seek fulfillment in some faraway heaven.

This objection overlooks the truth that man's quest for his identity starts from the experience of love. If love is the starting point of the human quest, then man depends on a revelation—the revelation of love—in order to find happiness. Because man's quest itself begins in love, this revelation does not blindside him like a thunderbolt out of the blue. Rather human experience is open to this revelation, tends toward it, and is an expectation of it—not in some future Beyond, but in the midst of our everyday involvement with the world around us. We don't need to escape mundane human life in order to experience love's radiance and light; we can bathe in its warmth right in the midst of our humdrum daily occupations.

Now, Christianity, like love, is a revelation that man can't contrive on his own. Moreover, Christian revelation, like love, happens right in the midst of our earthly space and time: "And the Word became flesh and dwelt among us" (John 1:14). This similarity between the human experience of love and the experience of faith in God's revelation suggests a further step in our argument: Christianity is itself the fullness of the revelation of love. In the words of the apostle John: "So we know and believe the love God has for us" (1 John

4:16). The manifestation of love John speaks of happens in Christ's life, death, and Resurrection. This is why Pope Benedict XVI can write: "It is [in the contemplation of the pierced side of Christ] that our definition of love must begin" (*DCE*, 12).

We can sum up what we have said so far by quoting two passages from John Paul II side by side. In the first passage, John Paul describes man's need for love in stark terms: "Man cannot live without love. He remains a being that is incomprehensible for himself, his life is senseless, if love is not revealed to him, if he does not encounter love" (*RH*, 10). The second passage, a citation from the Second Vatican Council that recurs often in John Paul II's writings, sums up the core experience of faith: "The truth is that only in the mystery of the incarnate Word does the mystery of man take on light . . . Christ, the final Adam, by the revelation of the mystery of the Father and His love, fully reveals man to man himself and makes his supreme calling clear" (*GS*, 22).

For John Paul II, then, life revolves around the revelation of love. But the same is true of faith, which hinges on Christ's revelation of the fullness of love. So there is no opposition between human experience and the experience of faith. Rather, there is a continuity between them, and each illuminates the other. On the one hand, we cannot understand Christian faith without understanding man's encounter with love. On the other hand, the human experience of love points toward a fullness that comes to light only in the encounter with Christ. Wonder culminates in faith's response to Christ's revelation of the fullness of love:

In reality, the name for that deep wonder at man's worth and dignity is the Gospel, that is to say: the Good News. It is also called Christianity. This wonder determines the Church's mission in the world and, perhaps even more so, "in the modern world." This wonder, which is also a conviction and a certitude . . . is closely connected with Christ. (*RH*, 10)

Leaving everyday life behind, or saying no to human experience and happiness, then, is *not* the prerequisite for preaching the Gospel. Quite the contrary: Christianity is the way of love, the answer to all of man's questions and the great Yes to his deepest longings. In his first encyclical, *Redemptor Hominis* (The Redeemer of Man), John Paul II taught that man is the way of the Church, while also insisting that man's way is the way of love. This way of love is in turn the path Benedict XVI proposes for the Church in *his* first encyclical, *Deus Caritas Est*. The continuity between the way of man and the way of love also reflects the continuity between the pontificates of John Paul II and his successor.

CHRISTIANITY IS THE WAY OF LOVE

Our aim in the rest of this book is to substantiate the claims we've made so far about the convergence between human experience, love, and Christian revelation. We want to show, then, that love is the way of man and that the mission of the Church is precisely to manifest the truth of love in the world.

This task, though simply stated, is not without its difficulties. The first problem arises as soon as we consider the different, and even contradictory, meanings that attach themselves to the word "love." We use it to praise the noblest of sacrifices—but we also use it to excuse a man who abandons his wife and children for another woman: "he did it for love." Clearly, many of us have never progressed beyond a rudimentary notion of love as an essentially selfish emotional rush. The protagonist of French writer Georges Bernanos's novel *The Diary of a Country Priest* puts us on our guard against the dangerous ambiguity that colors our talk about love. Addressing a person who invoked love as the motivation for her selfish actions, the country priest responds: "Don't use that word, 'love' . . . You've lost the right, and doubtless the power."⁴

But even supposing that we define the word "love" properly, we still have to ask whether our proclamation of its power to disclose the meaning of our lives isn't a bit overblown: Could love *really* be the answer to the riddle of our whole existence? Can we really say that love is the foundation of reality, the final explanation of history? Or is our enterprise in this book no better than a naive attempt to explain the meaning of life through the prism of a mere emotion? Aren't we in any case taking love too seriously? Doesn't our earnest talk about revelation rob love of its playfulness and spontaneity?

Our basic approach to these and similar objections depends on a key insight: *The fate of love is bound up with the fate of Christianity.* On the one hand, when we lose sight of the meaning and importance of love, we become blind to the presence of God in the midst of our experience, and we can no longer perceive him except as an alien intruder, or even as an enemy of human nature. On the other hand, without the light of God's love revealed in Christ, we eventually lose our ability to understand even the fullness of human love itself. If both of these claims are true—and we hope to show that they are— then recovering the connection between love and Christianity is the best way to answer the sorts of questions we posed just now.

John Paul II is a perfect guide in this recovery, because the late pope learned to love human love through his work with families as a young priest, and drew his rich understanding of the relationship between men and women from the mutual illumination of divine revelation and human experience. Following in John Paul's footsteps, we propose to train the twin beacons of love and faith on the path that leads man to the fullness of his true identity. Our account of love's journey in light of John Paul II's theology of the body will unfold in three stages: from the initial call to love, through all the obstacles that hinder our attempts to answer it, to love's final, longed-for fulfillment. In the first part of the book ("Encountering Love") we will examine how love is revealed to us and how this revelation opens a path for us to follow. The second part ("The Redemption of the Heart") will deal with the difficulties we encounter on this path of love and explain how Christ offers us the strength to overcome them. The third part ("The Beauty of Love") will conclude the book with a reflection on how Christ leads us, whether in marriage or in consecrated virginity, toward the fullness of love in heaven.

PART I

ENCOUNTERING
LOVE:
THE EXPERIENCE
OF THE BODY
AND THE
REVELATION OF
LOVE

CHAPTER I

THE BODY MANIFESTS THE PERSON

We began our journey of reflection in this book with John Paul II's identification of the key difference between man and the rest of the visible creation: "The rushing stream cannot wonder . . . but man can wonder!" (*RT*, 8). This wonder, we went on to see, is called forth by the richness of our experience of life—especially by the experience of love. Our task now is to ponder the indispensable role the body plays in this many-faceted experience of wonder.

EXPERIENCE AND MEANING

We all face the temptation to let life's current carry us along—to "go with the flow" without any resistance. But if we simply let a flood of experiences wash over us, we are in danger of losing the meaning of our lives. A recent survey of teenagers in Southampton, United Kingdom, revealed that this danger is anything but purely theoreti-

cal. The respondents, it turned out, possessed only a limited vocabulary to express the emotional quality of their response to the world.
These teens suffered from what has been called "affective illiteracy":
the inability to grasp and express the meaning of the experiences
generated in us by our encounter with the world around us.[1]

It isn't enough, then, simply to let our experiences wash over us.
We need to plumb their depth. This exploration isn't a matter of
"sampling" as many possibilities as we can, or of ratcheting up the
volume of our existence, but requires us to ask ourselves questions
such as these: Are we capable of distinguishing between experiences
that build up our happiness and experiences that tear it down? Are
we able to discern in our experiences something like a compass for
our life's journey? In a word: *Are we capable of perceiving the meaning
of our experiences?*

We tend to put experience and meaning in separate boxes. We
have already seen why this won't work. When man experiences the
world, he necessarily experiences himself in the process. For the
same reason, man's experience of the world always involves an at least
minimal search for the meaning of his life. The sight of a majestic
mountainscape doesn't just reveal the wonder of creation; it also af-
fords us an opportunity to lay hold of our innate capacity for beauty
and wonder. Since the question of man emerges from our contact
with the world, experience always goes together with a search for
meaning. Even the refusal to embark on this search is an answer to
the question of meaning.

> We had the experience, we missed the meaning
> And approach to the meaning restores the experience
> In a different form.[2]

These lines from T. S. Eliot's poem "The Dry Salvages" underscore the point that meaning is not foreign to experience. Quite the contrary, meaning *is an integral part of* experience. So much so, in fact, that meaning makes our experience properly human in the first place. John Paul II's insight into this unity of meaning and experience guided his reflection on the theology of the body, which begins with an effort to recollect the authentic "feel" of man's experience in light of its deepest meaning. In a word, the pope guides us through the labyrinth of our lives using the golden thread of what he calls *"original experiences."* So what is an "original experience"?

THE ORIGINAL EXPERIENCE

John Paul II invites us to seek the true depth of our experience. Actually, it is Christ himself who first entrusted this task to us. When the Pharisees asked him, "Is it lawful to divorce one's wife for any cause?" (Matt. 19:3), he didn't list minimum sufficient grounds for divorce, but went instead to the heart of the matter: Is it really possible to love another person forever? The Pharisees clearly assumed that the answer was no. This assumption reflects their (and our) hardness of heart, and it speaks volumes about man's alienation from the root of his experience of love.

Christ came to retrieve and fulfill this root of love, and he therefore replies to the Pharisees by telling them to reread the creation accounts in the book of Genesis. He thus invites his questioners to recover the depth of their experience in the mirror of God's original intention for human love. John Paul II takes Christ at his word. As we know, Genesis presents two different accounts of creation, and

John Paul II devotes considerable attention to both. Let's start with his reflections on the first narrative (Gen. 1:1–2:3), which lights up the true shape of our experience of everyday life in the blaze of God's Word.

The biblical text unfurls the rich tapestry of creation with all of its color and variety. It places man at the summit of the whole created world and underscores his special privilege of being made in the image and likeness of God. The words "image and likeness" signal the overture to the covenant between God and man in the Bible. They tell us that from the beginning man is the one to whom God addresses his Word and whose special status lies in his capacity to answer this divine call.

The Bible's affirmation of man's dignity as the "image and likeness of God," which comes at the end of the first creation account, calls for further commentary, because it still leaves open how man is meant to respond to the Creator. Answering this question is the job that falls to the second creation story (Gen. 2:4–3:24), which can thus be seen as the natural continuation of the first. After we've listened to the creative voice of God in the first account, we perceive man's answering voice in the second. The second creation narrative enables us to rediscover the inner experience through which we are to respond to the Creator's call.

In other words, the second creation account shifts the point of view of the story: Now it's man who speaks and reveals his interior world. This account doesn't just observe man from the outside; it presents the human journey of wonderment from man's own point of view. By putting us in man's shoes as he was in the beginning, the second creation account unfolds the "original experiences" we spoke of just now. John Paul II sums up these experiences under the three headings of "original solitude," "original unity," and "original nakedness."

Before going on to describe these original experiences, though, we should stop to ask ourselves whether we really *can* describe them, or even have any access to them at all. How can anyone retrieve events that supposedly took place at the very dawn of history? Even if we could do so, we would still face a further difficulty: Aren't the original experiences John Paul II describes permeated by a purity and innocence sin has extinguished in our hearts? How can experiences belonging to a sunken past help us attain happiness here and now?

Fortunately, man's original experiences of the beginning have in fact never been totally lost. Two images help illustrate the abiding presence of the beginning in the midst of our everyday reality.

The first image comes from J. R. R. Tolkien's *The Silmarillion*, which opens with a "creation myth" that compares God's creative design to a piece of music.[3] As Tolkien goes on to relate, Melkor, the dark angel, becomes jealous of God's creative power and tries to introduce a discordant note of his own into the celestial orchestra. Yet, as God reminds Melkor, even this disharmony cannot destroy the pattern of the original music. On the contrary, even Melkor's rebellion will be woven (against his intention) into the final master theme all creation will sing to God's glory.

Similarly, we can compare the three original experiences John Paul II refers to with a primordial music that, while distorted through sin, has never completely been destroyed by it. If we listen inattentively, we will hear only noise. If, however, we keep silent and turn our ear to the hidden pattern beneath the noise, we can still discern the original melody that reflects the Creator's wise design. Actually, it's only because the original harmony still resonates in the background that we can hear the dissonance as the disruption it is.

Another way of putting this is that the original experiences are not "original" only in the sense that they happened at the beginning of human history. We call the original experiences "original" because they lie at the basis of every other experience and provide the theme for every other music we compose with our lives. Our use of "original," then, has the same double meaning as the Greek word *arché*, which signifies both a temporal beginning and the foundations of a building. This leads us to the second image that illustrates the continuing accessibility of man's original experiences.

As the facade of Saint Peter's Basilica was being cleaned recently in preparation for the Jubilee of the year 2000, the workers were surprised by the green color of the marble surrounding the central windows. Some even thought that the chemical agents used to clean the building were destroying the marble's original color. Consultation of the original plans for the basilica, however, brought to light that this green was indeed the true color of the stone. It's just that it had been covered in grime for so long that no one could recollect its original appearance.

A similar grime builds up over our attitude toward life. As children, we live close to the original experiences of Adam and Eve, but as we grow up their freshness is progressively polluted by layers of routine and mechanization. The French philosopher Gabriel Marcel once said that we are the bureaucrats of our own existence, who have buried our original contact with life under mountains of paperwork and procedures that impair our capacity to discern the human drama lying beneath them.[4]

If Marcel is right, then the child is closer to man's original experiences, but the adult has almost forgotten them (but not quite). Since the original experiences hover as a vague memory on the borders of our adult awareness, the effort to recover them demands something like a retrieval and healing of these almost obliterated childhood memories. This doesn't mean that we should turn our back on adulthood. Rather our task is to integrate the child's primal contact with life into our adult consciousness. This retrieval unlocks the deep meaning of Jesus's command: "Unless you turn and become like children, you will not enter the kingdom of heaven" (see Matt. 18:3).

Of course, only the encounter with Christ enables a *total* recovery of our original experiences. By the same logic, since the Church preserves the living memory of Christ's presence, it is she who also keeps alive the memory of the beginning. As John Paul II wrote in his last book, *Memory and Identity*:

> What is at issue here is not only the mystery of Christ. In him, it is the mystery of man that is revealed from the beginning. There is probably no other text on the origins of man so simple and yet so complete as that contained in the first three chapters of the Book of Genesis. Here not only do we find an account of the creation of man as male and female, but his particular vocation in the universe is made abundantly clear ... The Church preserves within herself the memory of man's history from the beginning: the memory of his creation, his vocation, his elevation, and his fall. Within this essential framework the whole of human history, the history of Redemption, is written. The Church is a mother who, like Mary, treasures in her heart the story of her children, making all their problems her own.[5]

John Paul II invites us, then, on a quest for the original experiences that make sense out of our lives and point man toward his true fulfillment. He calls us to accompany Adam in his search for his identity, for Adam's search is ours, too. The reader should bear in mind that we will be using the name "Adam" in three different ways in the rest of this book. First of all, "Adam" means man in the inclusive sense of "human being"; "Adam" in this first generally accepted meaning refers to every member of the human race, whether man or woman. Second, "Adam" sometimes refers explicitly to the male, whereas "Eve" stands for the female. Whenever we use the name "Adam" in this second sense, we will try to make it clear that he cannot be understood apart from the woman who, while different from him, is his equal in dignity. Third, "Adam" is a character in several of Karol Wojtyla's plays. Which of these three meanings "Adam" has at any given point in the discussion should be clear from the context.

ORIGINAL SOLITUDE

John Paul II's *Roman Triptych* describes man's search for meaning that begins with the experience of wonder. This search is a journey to the Source:

> If you want to find the source,
> you have to go up, against the current.
> Break through, search, don't yield,
> you know it must be here somewhere.
> Where are you? . . . Source, where are you?! (*RT*, 9)

Having grasped this point, we are ready to turn to the second creation account in the book of Genesis, which retrieves the deepest meaning of human experience in the light of man's relation to this Source, whose freshness John Paul II invites us to taste with our own lips.

The Bible relates that God forms Adam from the clay of the ground, imparts to him the breath of life, and then says: "It is not good that the man should be alone" (Gen. 2:18). According to Genesis, then, Edenic man, though surrounded by every kind of plant and animal, felt alone. Adam experienced what John Paul II calls "original solitude."

Original solitude doesn't just mean that Adam lacked Eve. Original solitude is not a mere deficit that is subsequently filled out by the creation of the woman. For John Paul II, the experience of original solitude remains even after Eve's appearance in the Garden. Original solitude is an essential experience of the human being, both male and female; it remains at the root of every other human experience and so accompanies man throughout his whole life's journey. Let's look more closely at how original solitude shapes human existence.

The term "original solitude" underscores man's uniqueness when compared with the other kinds of beings that surround him, which do not belong to the same order of magnitude as he does. Original solitude is thus another way of expressing man's special dignity, which rests on the basis of his unique privilege of being fashioned in the image and likeness of God as his partner in a dialogue of love. Man is the only living being on earth whom God addresses as a father addresses his son. In a word, original solitude is man's special relationship with his Creator.

John Paul II explores this aspect of original solitude in *Roman Triptych*. For man, the pope writes, "it is not enough to exist and go his way." Why not? Because man is "alone in his wonderment, among many beings incapable of wonder" (*RT*, 8). The wonderment that prompts man to seek his own identity is both a discovery and an expression of his original solitude before God. In the words of Saint Augustine: "You have made us for yourself, and our heart is restless until it rests in you."[6]

According to the biblical account, God molds Adam out of the dust of the ground and places him in the middle of the Garden of Eden, where there is abundant water and vegetation—tokens of God's care for his creature. These images vividly illustrate man's solidarity with the material creation. Scripture uses the term "flesh" (in Hebrew, *basar*) to designate this membership in the material universe. "Flesh" is not merely the physical side of man. Rather, the whole man is "flesh" insofar as he exists in relationship with nature and his fellow human beings.

Since he is "flesh," Adam's discovery of his original solitude before God is not the result of some effortful introspection, but of an immediate encounter with the world that (according to the Bible) he gains by tilling the garden and naming the animals that God brings before him. A crucially important corollary follows from this: Original solitude is revealed in the human body. We don't do justice to original solitude by fleeing from the body, but by refining our lived experience of bodily life and learning from the inside what it is like to be a living body.

I AM MY BODY

The human body expresses man's original solitude and witnesses to his superiority over the other animals. But how does the human body actually display the difference that sets man apart from the rest of the physical creation?[7] If man's body is part of the material world, how can it also reveal his unique dignity at the same time?

It's tempting in today's scientistic climate to reduce man to the set of natural processes that all material entities have (or supposedly have) in common. In his play *Radiation of Fatherhood*, Karol Wojtyla expresses the angst that this reductionism generates in the human soul. Adam, a character who stands for Everyman, exclaims, "I have toiled unceasingly to reach [my own identity] but have often thought with horror that it was disappearing, blurred among the processes of history, in which what matters is numbers, mass" (*RF*, 335). In reality, our intuition that we are much more than "numbers and mass" cannot be gainsaid. "Numbers retreat before Man,"[8] the pope has written, because his experience of the body repels every attempt to reduce his physical existence to the common material structures with which the natural sciences busy themselves. So what is the distinctive character that sets the human body apart from the rest of the world?

Reductionism derives a certain superficial plausibility from the fact that we can talk about our bodies as if they were material objects. For instance, I can say that my body "belongs" to me, and I can refer to "my body" in apparently the same way as I talk about "my car" or "my dog." This way of talking about the body isn't totally false. After all, I can use my body (or parts thereof) as a tool; for example, I can turn a screw with the help of a screwdriver, but I can also try to do the same job with my hand. Nevertheless, a crucial difference remains. While there is always a distance between us and our belongings, there is no distance between us and our bodies. We can be dispossessed of our belongings and go on living happy lives, but we can't be dispossessed of our bodies without ceasing to be. The body, then, is not just another item in our stock of possessions, but rather the foundation of our very capacity to possess anything in the first place. Similarly, the body is not just another tool in our toolkit; it establishes the very possibility of our using instruments at all: I can wield a hammer only because I first have hands, just as I can peer through a microscope only because I first have eyes.

There's something incomplete and potentially misleading in expressions such as "I have a body." Since the body is neither a possession nor a tool, I need to add: *I am my body* (see *TOB*, 147; 166). This does not mean that I am mere matter or that I can be reduced to material processes. It actually means just the opposite: My body is personal; it is part of the definition of who I am, and any answer to the question of my identity has to take my body into account. The body is not some object "out there," but is suffused with personal meaning from the inside out.

Let's try to delve a little more deeply into our mysterious relationship with our bodies. Suppose I see several objects placed before me: a computer, a telephone, a picture hanging on the wall. What is the difference between them and my body, by which I'm experiencing them? Unlike inanimate objects, the living body has the capacity to feel. The picture hangs on the wall, but it does not feel the wall; I sit in my chair looking at the picture, but I also feel the chair. Because inanimate objects do not feel, they are always external to themselves; they have an *inside* (you can cut or break them open), but no *interiority* (they don't notice that they're being cut into or broken). Of course, the living body also has an external dimension like inanimate objects. This explains why we can talk about "our bodies" as if they were outside us. Nevertheless, even when we look at our bodies in this more external way, we do so from the deeper point of view that comes with interiority or inwardness. Before the body is something I *have*, it just *is* the way I "feel" the world, am present to it, and participate in it.[9]

An important corollary of all this is that "no man is an island," and none of us can think of himself as an isolated individual. For the body tells us a different story. It teaches us that we are open toward the world from the inside, whether we like it or not. It brings home to us that we are always in relationship with others, and that this relationship touches the very core of who we are. Our bodies immerse us in the world prior to any choice on our part, yet the fact that this immersion is not chosen does not destroy our dignity. Rather it empowers us to perform the action that reveals our special status as human beings: to experience wonder in our encounter with other people and things.

THE BODY IS A HOME

Since the body is more than an object or an instrument, we need a better picture to describe it. The image of a home is suitable. The home is not just a *house* to buy or sell, but the intimate dwelling where we are truly ourselves. It is the "habitat" where human life is transmitted and nurtured. The home supports human life, and anyone who has a home brings it with him wherever he goes, because it is part of his identity.

Thinking of the body as a home in this sense helps us understand man's relationship with the world, because, like the home, the body is the dwelling in which we receive other things and persons as our guests. The image of hospitality reminds us that our original experience of the body is neither sheer passivity before the world nor sheer power over it, but *receptivity* toward it. Receptivity is neither pure activity nor pure passivity but partakes of the best of both worlds. On the more "passive side," receptivity responds to the things or people that step into my life unasked; on the more "active side," receptivity mobilizes my full "hospitality," just as a good host is not a doormat but attends to his guests with a generous measure of spontaneity and imaginativeness.

The first thing familiarity with the language of the body teaches us is how to be hospitable to the world around us. This is why experiencing the body as a home is crucial to restoring a proper relationship to the environment. Modern man's estrangement from his own body—and so his homelessness in nature—is at the root of the ecological problems our society currently faces. The word "ecology" comes from the Greek work *oikos*, "home," and the theology of the body is a first step toward the recovery of the world as that home.

The body is a great liberator that frees us from the isolation of the lonely ego that is (at most) certain only of its own existence. Right from the outset, the body plunges man into the midst of the world, opens him to it in wonder, and enables him to respond to it in the same spirit of amazement. This embodied participation in the world is in turn the root from which every other human experience grows. In the next two sections, we'll explore how even our *self-consciousness* and *freedom* grow from this root as expressions of this hospitality the body teaches us to exercise toward the world around us.

THE BODY AND HUMAN IDENTITY

Although original solitude sets man apart from the rest of the visible creation, it doesn't cut him off from the rest of the world. On the contrary, if man shrinks from the world and takes refuge in the fortress of his isolated subjectivity, he loses the key that unlocks the depth dimension of his own being. Man's self-consciousness—his awareness of his true dignity—comes to fruition only in a gesture of hospitality toward the world that comes to knock at the door of his senses.

The body is man's openness to the world. Nevertheless, the world never totally fills the receptive capacity of the bodily home in which man welcomes it. This does not mean that the world is defective. The reason the world doesn't fill us completely is not that it is flawed. The point is simply that the world's perfection is designed to manifest God, in whom alone man's heart finds rest. This suggests a crucial aspect of original solitude: the capacity to find God in the midst of the world.

Let us put together the two conclusions we just reached. First, man is aware of himself only in his encounter with the world. Second, this encounter with the world is open toward an infinite horizon, toward the encounter with God. It follows from this that *man is aware of himself when he is in dialogue with God*, when God addresses him and talks with him, as he spoke with Adam in the cool of the day in the Garden of Eden. This connection allows us to complete the image of the body as a home. Since man's openness to the world reaches into the infinite, we can think of the body, not just as a home, but also as a temple. The New Testament compares the body to a temple indwelt by the Holy Spirit (see 1 Cor. 6:19).

According to the Bible, man's special relation to the Creator begins with his conception and birth. As the potter molds the clay, so God forms man's body in his mother's womb (see Jer. 1:5). Our bodies remind us that our origin is not in ourselves, and reveal the true Origin of our life instead: "For thou didst form my inward parts, thou didst knit me together in my mother's womb" (Ps. 139:13). The fundamental experience of mortality confirms the same truth at the opposite end of life's spectrum. Man differs from the animals precisely because death is a *problem* for him. Unlike all other earthly creatures, man wonders about the meaning of his impending end. This awareness of our future death, rooted as it is in the body, reveals our original solitude and teaches us to look to God as our true Goal, just as birth teaches us to regard him as our true Origin. Thanks to the body, man's life is a journey whose origin and ultimate destination is the Creator.

FREEDOM IN THE BODY

Man's bodily engagement with reality is not a passive affair in which he merely registers data that bombard him from the outside world. Man is a receptive being, but his receptivity is not the pliability of a jellyfish. It is an active readiness to welcome the world around him. The active nature of this receptivity naturally raises the question of freedom, which we express through our answer to the primordial call of the real.

At first sight, it might seem that freedom has nothing to do with the body. Indeed, it's quite common nowadays to hear the claim that, in order to be free, we need to get rid of the limitations of space and time that our bodies inevitably place on us. If we attend to the nature of the body, however, we realize that it is the basis of our freedom—not in spite of its limitations, but *through* them. Our bodies do not constrain our freedom; they make us truly free in the first place.

Think of a musician. His chief means of expression and communication is his musical artistry. Now suppose we told him that he is enslaved by the physical laws of sound and that the air transmitting the notes he plays is an obstacle to his music! Suppose, further, that we urged him to imagine some much more rapid means of conveying sound that would entail proportionately less resistance to his playing. He would surely reply that we are victims of a serious misunderstanding. What we are calling "hindrances," he would explain, are not obstacles to his art or his ability to communicate by means of it. On the contrary, they grant him the very possibility of expressing himself musically and so enable him to achieve communion with the rest of the world through his art.[10]

What we have said about the musician can be applied to every artist, whether it be the sculptor who carves a statue out of marble or the painter who mixes the colors he needs for a particular canvas. The sculptor would never complain that the marble is a "limitation," nor would the painter resent his colors as an "impediment" to his art. Like the musician, both the sculptor and the painter are happy to conform to the medium they work with even as they transform it. Such artists know, in fact, that their conformity to the medium is precisely *how* they transform the medium in the first place.

We said just now that our bodies enable our freedom. The example of the artist—whether musician, sculptor, or painter—suggests what kind of freedom the body makes possible for us: the creative freedom to communicate beauty. The body is like an artist's expressive medium, which is not shapeless raw material, but *is* the work of art, waiting to be drawn out of the marble, the colors, or the musical notes. If human freedom were disembodied, it might have more room to play with hypothetical possibilities, but it would be unable to create anything beautiful or to share such beauty with the rest of the world.

Human freedom is a capacity for creative communication. It is fittingly rooted in the body, because the body opens us to participation in reality. This is what Pope Benedict XVI means when he speaks of the body as the "region of freedom" where real engagement with the world occurs (*DCE*, 5). Benedict's words are a warning to avoid confusing freedom with an absence of limits. Freedom is the ability to be open to the world, to receive the new things we encounter in it, and to respond to their call with genuine creativity.

Life is a gift, and this gift deserves to be received ever anew in freedom from the Creator, who formed our bodies in our mother's womb. His call is written into our bodies, and our freedom is an answer to this summons. By the same token, the body sets our freedom on a journey toward divine transcendence. *Fecisti nos ad te*, said Saint Augustine in his *Confessions*: You made us *"toward"* yourself.[11] The body is like a road on which our freedom journeys to God and grows in relationship with him. In the words of John Paul II, "God has assigned the body to man as a task" (*TOB*, 360).

FREEDOM, RESPONSIBILITY, AND WORK

The body enables man to respond creatively to the world and to God—and to respond is to be responsible. There is no true freedom without responsibility.

We learn to appreciate the link between freedom and responsibility through work. We could even define work as man's way of giving the material world a share in the dignity of the human body. To work is to give the world a human shape.

Nevertheless, because we work in our bodies, our labor isn't purely external to us. Nor is its value simply the sum total of what we produce. The *quality* of work is not measured only by the *quantity* of the objects our work may produce. John Paul II, who put in countless hours of manual labor in a Polish factory, was very sensitive to the impact of work on *the worker himself* and on the development of his character—an impact the pope called the "subjective" dimension of work.[12] Because man works in his body, whenever he transforms the world through work, he is also transforming and molding *himself.* Now, since man's life is a journey toward God, the work by which he shapes his life is a kind of "liturgy" (which comes from the Greek word *leitourgia*, meaning "work of the people"). To work is to shape the world into a reflection of our relationship with God; it is to incorporate the world into our worship. Every human action, every work man performs, no matter how humble, has a liturgical dignity.

SUMMING UP:
THE BODY AND ITS LANGUAGE

Saint Paul sums up what we've said about the dignity of the body when he writes: "Glorify God in your body" (1 Cor. 6:20). The great mystic Saint Symeon the New Theologian (949–1022) powerfully reinforces Paul's amazement at the grandeur of the human body:

> O wonder! I am vigilant, I am full of respect for myself, of reverence and of fear, as I would be were I before You; I do not know what to do, I am seized by fear, I do not know where to sit, where to go, where to put these members which are yours; in what deeds, in what works shall I use them, these amazing divine marvels![13]

If this chapter has achieved its main purpose, then the reader will set it down with a deeper appreciation of his own body, which is not an insignificant piece of "meat," but the vehicle of a revelation. This revelation tells us of our solitude amidst our fellow creatures, just as it brings home to us that our origin and destiny are in the hands of the Creator and that our life is a journey toward him. The word "revelation" suggests a further point whose implications we will unfold throughout the remainder of this book. One of the most original insights of John Paul II's theology, in fact, is that the body has a proper "language" in which the Creator expresses himself. We are all familiar with the experience of nonverbal communication that is called "body language," but the pope is drawing our attention to an even more basic phenomenon: The body is meaningful even before we perform any special gestures with it, for it is the very "grammar" of the original experiences that define our humanity. We've already examined the first of these experiences: original solitude. The next chapter will accordingly explore how the language of the body speaks love in the encounter between man and woman that is the core of what John Paul II calls "original unity." It's only when he stands face-to-face with Eve that Adam clearly realizes and joyfully expresses the wonder of his existence. For it's only in meeting Eve that he fully understands how his body leads him to God.

CHAPTER 2

SEXUAL DIFFERENCE:
THE VOCATION
TO LOVE

THE PREVIOUS CHAPTER FOCUSED ON THE INITIAL STAGE
in Adam's quest for his identity, which begins when the body reveals
the world to him in all its mystery and sets him on a journey of wonder. Adam knows that his trip begins and ends with God, but how
is he to make the journey back to the Source? What concrete shape
should his partnership with God take? Adam's quest for his identity
remains "on hold" so long as these questions are unanswered.

Adam stands poised on the brink of an event that will reshape his
whole existence. This event is his encounter with Eve, and it alone
reveals the true depth of his being to him. John Paul II calls this next
step in man's search for the Absolute *original unity.* Let us accompany Adam as he continues his journey into original unity, without
forgetting that his journey is also ours.

ENCOUNTERING LOVE: "THIS AT LAST IS BONE OF MY BONES AND FLESH OF MY FLESH" (GEN. 2:23)

The first point we have to stress is that Adam is not the engineer or designer of Eve, whose surprising presence in his life exceeds his imagination. Love is always a revelation that we cannot plan or produce, but that has to take us by surprise. The Bible uses the image of sleep to express Adam's inability to produce Eve: God casts Adam into a deep slumber and then directly forms the woman's body from the man's. Similarly, it is God himself who presents the new-formed woman to her husband as a suitable helpmate. No wonder, then, that at the sight of Eve Adam cries out with joy: "This at last!" He rejoices because Eve brings home to him how abundantly reality exceeds all of his expectations. Adam stands before a new human person whose very presence enriches and enlarges the horizon of his life's journey.

"This at last is bone of my bones and flesh of my flesh" (Gen. 2:23). Notice Adam's graphically realistic talk of "bones" and "flesh." The interpersonal encounter that reveals love happens precisely in the body. To exist in the body, we said, means to be open to, and to participate in, reality. This bodily openness in turn makes love possible, for to love is to share your world with another person who is flesh of your flesh and bone of your bones. John Paul II's name for this mutual indwelling in one another's experience is "original unity."

Let's stop for a moment to ponder the significance of this new step in the gradual revelation of reality through the body. The last chapter explained how Adam is present in, and interacts with, the world through the body. We can now add that the body, with its emotions and feelings, enables him to enter Eve's world and to see it with her eyes. The body is Adam's bridge to union with Eve, just as her body is her bridge to union with him. At one point in *The Jeweler's Shop*, Andrew uses an analogy to express how the body enables man and woman to share their respective inner worlds with each other. Speaking of Teresa, who has just accepted his proposal of marriage, Andrew says: "Today I see that my country is also her country/ and, after all, I dreamed of throwing a bridge" (*JS*, 31).

Admittedly, the body can also be a barrier that cuts us off from others. We can learn to lie with the body, just as we lie with words. Even so, we always retain at least a dim awareness that such falsehood contradicts the very nature of the body itself, and that by using the body to lie we are forcing it against the grain. According to the book of Genesis, the body is made to serve as a bridge uniting persons, not as a barrier separating them; its purpose is not to exclude others but to give them a chance to experience reality "in our shoes." Pushing this idea even further, John Paul describes love as a mutual indwelling that enables each of the lovers to inhabit the other's inner space. In *The Jeweler's Shop*, for example, Andrew portrays his love as "a strange persistence of Teresa in me," a "strange resonance." Speaking of her love for Stefan in the same play, Anna exclaims:

> Is it not too terrible a thing
> to have committed the walls of my interior
> to a single inhabitant
> who could disinherit my self
> and somehow deprive me of my place in it! (*JS*, 48)

Let's pause for a moment to anticipate a point that we'll develop more amply later on in this chapter. The emotions enable us to participate in one another's inner lives. It goes without saying that this

participation makes us vulnerable to the world around us. Nevertheless, we need to correct the common belief that such vulnerability
is an evil, or, at any rate, an inconvenient disturbance to be avoided
at any cost. It's true, of course, that everyone who loves sooner or
later gets hurt. Yet this very risk of pain has a positive side: By taking us out of ourselves, emotions are an entryway into the world of
other people. By coming to share in that world, we learn to live more
richly. And this is surely a risk worth taking.

LOVE'S NEW CREATION

Our journey in this chapter has brought us to the point of recog-
nizing how the body ushers man into a new dimension of existence
through union with another person. This new mode of existence
touches man's identity so deeply that John Paul II compares it to a
second creation. In fact, the pope goes so far as to say that the creation of man isn't complete until he exists as male and female and the
two are one. The achievement of this original unity fills the one la-
cuna that, according to the creation account, still remained in Eden:
"It is not good that the man should be alone."[1] The divine hands
have finished their masterpiece, shaping man into the unity of two
beings that John Paul II calls a "communion of persons."

The pope's interpretation of Genesis rings true to our experience:
To know love is to be created anew. By the same token, to love others
is, in a sense, to create them in our turn. After all, to love someone
isn't just to appreciate his good qualities; it is to rejoice in his very
being in the first place. To love is to say: "It is good that you exist!"
Just as God declared that his creation was "very good" after having

fashioned man, so, too, when we affirm our loved ones we are sharing in God's work of giving them existence.[2]

In *The Jeweler's Shop*, Karol Wojtyla uses a lovely image to illustrate how love re-creates two people as one. Anna, whose marriage
is in the throes of a profound crisis, goes to the Jeweler (who represents God in the play) in order to sell him her wedding ring. Here, in
Anna's own words, is what happens next:

> The jeweler examined the workmanship, weighed the ring
> for a long time in his fingers and looked
> into my eyes . . . put the ring on the scales . . .
> then said, "This ring does not weigh anything,
> the needle does not move from zero
> and I cannot make it show
> even a milligram.
> Your husband must be alive
> in which case neither of your rings, taken separately,
> will weigh anything—only both together will register.
> My jeweler's scales
> have this peculiarity
> that they weigh not the metal
> but man's entire being and fate." (*JS*, 52)

Adam's journey has taken a somewhat surprising twist. For it
turns out that his relationship with Eve is the key to answering the
question of his identity (and the same is true of her with respect to
him). Adam's quest has obliged him to enlarge the circle of his consciousness to welcome the inner life of Eve (and vice versa). He has
learned the truth that love is "one of those processes in the universe

which bring a synthesis, unite what was divided, broaden and enrich what was limited and narrow" (*JS*, 26). Our task now is to flesh out our picture of the union of love in light of the complementarity of man and woman that is revealed in the body.

IDENTITY AND DIFFERENCE

In chapter 1 we compared our bodies to a home in which we welcome reality with an active hospitality. What we've learned so far in this chapter is that two bodies can become a common home, like two cities encircled by the same outer wall. In the words of Anna in *The Jeweler's Shop*, love is the act of entrusting "the walls of my interior / to [another] inhabitant" (*JS*, 48).

Love between man and woman is a communion that reforges the partners into a new unity. Communion, like the proverbial coin, has two sides, which we can call, respectively, "identity" and "difference." It goes without saying that identity and difference are at the center of every relationship with other people. The interplay of the two is essential to understanding the meaning of love in general. Nevertheless, this interplay attains a special degree of intensity in the love between man and woman, which lives in the interchange between the masculinity of the male body and the femininity of the female body. Let us consider each of the two dimensions of love in turn.

The book of Genesis, as we have seen, emphasizes God's sole initiative in creating Eve. The creation account thereby underscores the equal dignity of the first couple: Eve comes no less directly from God than Adam does. As John Paul II notes, Genesis 2 throws the equality of man and woman into relief through the very language it uses to refer to them. Most of us probably interpret the account of Eve's creation as the story of how a male human being named "Adam" got himself a wife. The picture changes somewhat when we learn that the name "Adam" is actually a play on the Hebrew word for earth: *hāʾadāmāh*. For, as John Paul II points out, it's only *after* the woman is created that the Bible first uses the Hebrew word for man in the sense of "male": '*iš*. When Eve appears on the scene, a new vocabulary suddenly emerges along with her: The text shifts from *hāʾadāmāh*, which emphasizes man's connection with the earth, to '*iš*, which it then immediately pairs with the word for "woman": '*iššāʰ*. Note the ingenious wordplay: The woman is called '*iššāʰ* because she has been taken from man, '*iš*.[3] It's as if Adam, hitherto a stand-in for "man" in the generic sense, had suddenly woken up to the fact that he is a *male*, whose existence makes sense only because he has a *female* counterpart (and we have to imagine Eve going through a similar experience in her turn).

Far from degrading women to an inferior status, then, the story of Adam's rib actually underscores that Adam and Eve, male and female, are identical in their dignity and their common humanity. To understand the significance of this identity, we need to think back to the experience of original solitude. Like Adam, Eve is incommensurable with the other bodies that surround her in the Garden. Like Adam's body, Eve's is open to the world, just as both of their bodies are equally characterized by total openness to the Absolute. Thus, when Adam says: "This at last . . . is flesh of my flesh," he is not just relating information about himself; he is affirming *Eve's* original solitude, the unique dignity that sets *her* apart from all the nonhuman entities populating the visible world. He is acknowledging the presence of someone with whom he can finally share a common world that is open to God. Adam's solitary quest has suddenly become a joint search with Eve, with each being a suitable helpmate for the other on their shared journey.

United in love, Adam and Eve are identical in their dignity as creatures open to God. Nevertheless, their union does not blur the difference between them, nor does it cancel the specific way in which each partner expresses the human dignity common to both. The fact that man and woman are different keeps them aware of their need for each another, reminding them that they are not complete in themselves. This difference (inscribed, remember, in the male and female body) is thus the beginning of a dynamic movement that takes each partner beyond him- or herself. It is an invitation to both to enrich their experience by learning to see the world from the other's point of view.

The sexual difference between male and female is man's great protection from the tragic fate of Narcissus, the character from Greek mythology who fell in love with his own reflection in a pool of water. Unlike Adam and Eve, Narcissus was incapable of being surprised by anything really new, for he was trapped in himself and his vain effort to capture his image reflected in the water. Here is how the Latin poet Ovid describes the sad fate of Narcissus:

> Catch not so fondly at a fleeting shade,
> And be no longer by yourself betray'd;
> It* borrows all it has from you alone,
> And it can boast of nothing of its own:
> With you it comes, with you it stays, and so
> Would go away, had you the power to go.[4]

* I.e., the image of Narcissus in the pool.

The book of Genesis uses the Hebrew word *kenegdo* to refer to Eve's identity as a helpmate who is similar to, and on a par with, Adam. Literally, *kenegdo* means "to stand face-to-face with another." Adam and Eve look each other in the eye, identical in humanity, yet different in their respective embodied expressions of humanity. Unlike Narcissus, Adam and Eve can't ignore their mutual difference, which liberates them from unfruitful navel-gazing, enabling them to get out of themselves and move toward each other.

It's important not to confuse the *difference* between man and woman with mere *diversity*. Human beings are indeed diverse, and this diversity is due to things such as race, social status, and a variety of talents or gifts. But diversity does not necessarily imply any inherent reference to other persons or entail any "being face-to-face with the other." A tall man does not need a short one in order to measure his height (a yardstick will do), just as we can understand the customs of African tribes without needing to compare them with how people live in Asia or Europe. The picture changes radically with sexuality, however. After all, sexuality makes no sense without the "face-to-face" relationship expressed by the Hebrew word *kenegdo*. Masculinity and femininity, then, are not only diverse. More important, they are *complementary*. The word "complementarity" designates the impossibility of understanding each sex without reference to the other and vice versa.

Angelo Cardinal Scola explains that the word "difference" comes from the Latin *differre*, which means "to bring the same thing to another place."[5] Difference, then, does not create mere diversity; it puts a distinct "spin" on the same thing. What the difference between man and woman "spins" is their relationship to the Absolute. Male and female are two different ways of living out the body's openness to transcendence. They are two complementary ways of experiencing the body as openness toward God. Masculinity and femininity "are, as it were, two different 'incarnations,' that is, two ways in which the same human being, created 'in the image of God' (Gen. 1:27), 'is a body' " (*TOB*, 157). By the same logic, masculinity and femininity shape how each partner journeys toward full understanding of his vocation to love.

THE HUMANITY OF EROS

The body is always either male or female, and it is the body that fleshes out for us the interplay of identity and difference between man and woman. We should stress that this interplay doesn't take place in some outer layer of our existence, but permeates the entire human person from inside out. "Love . . . has the taste of the whole man," we read in *The Jeweler's Shop* (*JS*, 60). Love resists every attempt to divide our life into a multitude of disjointed segments; love is the source of the unity we all long so deeply to experience within ourselves.

Pope Benedict XVI criticizes the modern tendency to fragmentation in his first encyclical, *Deus Caritas Est*. "The epicure Gassendi used to offer Descartes the humorous greeting: 'O Soul!' And Descartes would reply: 'O Flesh!' Yet it is neither the spirit alone nor the body alone that loves: It is man, the person, a unified creature composed of body and soul, who loves" (*DCE*, 5). Benedict's point in this passage is clear: We don't love only with our bodies or only with our souls. It's the whole person, body and soul, who loves. Love guarantees and expresses our unity as human persons. It certifies that we are one and guides us to the fulfillment of this unity in our lives.[6]

If we think of masculinity or femininity as the two "channels" through which human love flows, then being a man or a woman is much more than just an aspect or a segment of our existence. Rather, sexuality pervades our whole being from the inside out. Masculinity and femininity color how we participate in the world from top to bottom, and they accordingly pervade all of the actions by which we live out that participation.

Obviously, what we've just said flies in the face of the widespread tendency to pit sex against gender. Advocates of this opposition typically use the word "sex" to mean biological masculinity and femininity, the supposedly brute fact that you happen to be either male or female and to possess the corresponding reproductive organs. "Gender," by contrast, is used to indicate the concrete shape a given culture gives to biological sexuality through institutions such as the distribution of male and female "roles." Behind this stance, then, is the view that "sex" is a universal feature of human bodies, but that it is "merely biological," while "gender" is properly human but is culturally conditioned and so varies according to time and place.

The opposition between "sex" and "gender" typically bolsters the (false) claim that we can disjoin biology and humanity, which in fact are intimately and inextricably related. There is no such thing as "mere biology," nor is our biology "subhuman." On the contrary, biological masculinity and femininity, along with the body in which they are inscribed, are integral to what makes us truly human in the first place. As we saw in chapter 1, the body isn't just a brute given; it's a fundamental gift, a call to happiness that makes our freedom possible. By the same logic, attraction to the opposite sex, or *eros*, which "is somehow rooted in man's very nature" (*DCE*, 11), is an original call that enables the free response by which we build a genuinely human culture.

THE ASCENT OF LOVE

"My weight is my love. Wherever I am carried, my love is carrying me."[7] These words of Saint Augustine nicely encapsulate the idea that love is an attraction, a call rooted in our bodies that lights up our entire existence and invites us to set out on a new journey. The next question that logically arises at this point is: Where does this journey of love lead us? Our first step toward answering this question will be to examine the sensual desires and emotions that are rooted in our bodies; these are the first stirrings love's attraction awakens in us. As we will see, not even sensuality and emotion can be regarded as "subhuman," because they impel man and woman beyond them- selves and toward the Absolute.

Karol Wojtyla gives us a detailed description of sensuality and the emotional life in his book *Love and Responsibility*. What follows is a short tour through Wojtyla's analysis of these movements of love in this writing produced during his Polish years. After considering sen- sual desire, we will move on through feelings and emotions, to the affirmation of the value of the person, which affirmation responds to the beloved's unique dignity as a person willed into being by God.

Sensuality

The most basic level of erotic love for a person of the opposite sex is a rudimentary attraction that Karol Wojtyla calls "sensuality," a response to another's male or female body insofar as it is a "potential object of enjoyment" (*LR*, 160). In certain respects, this attraction is similar to the urge we feel toward food, drink, or any other object that satisfies our needs. Like these other impulses, sensuality lacks the ability to move us beyond our preoccupation with ourselves and our own needs. As Karol Wojtyla puts it, sensuality "in itself is quite blind to the person" of the opposite sex and is "oriented only towards [his or her] sexual value" (*LR*, 108).

Nevertheless, the comparison between sexual desires and other urges such as hunger and thirst is highly inadequate. Although it is itself "blind to the person," sensuality points beyond itself to a higher dimension of love. It contains a promise of happiness, even of a kind of ecstasy in the etymological sense of the word (which comes from the Greek *ek-stasis*, meaning "to be outside of oneself"). Of course, this promise of happiness cannot be fulfilled by sensuality alone, because sensuality by itself is unable to take us out of ourselves in the way that true ecstasy would demand. For the same reason, anyone who pursues sexual pleasure as an end in itself will eventually lose even the pleasure he seeks, for sensuality can give real fulfillment only when it is integrated into the broader dimension it points to but cannot attain by itself.

Feelings and Emotions

The natural tendency of sensuality is to direct us beyond sensuality to the world of the emotions. The emotions connect us with the beloved, whose personhood sensuality points to but cannot reach on its own. Consider the aspect of the emotional life that Wojtyla calls "sympathy." By his account, in fact, sympathy enables us to share in the interior world of the beloved; it is a jailbreak from the isolated prison of the ego, because it "keeps two people close together, binds them—even if they are physically far apart—to move in each other's orbit" (*LR*, 110). Sympathy is an indispensable step toward the communion of persons in love:

Sympathy brings people close together, into the same orbit, so that each is aware of the other's whole personality, and continually discovers that person in his own orbit. Precisely for this reason sympathy is that very important thing, the empirical and palpable manifestation of love between man and woman. It is thanks to sympathy that they are aware of their mutual love, and without sympathy they somehow lose their love and are left feeling once more that they are in a vacuum. (*LR*, 90)

Sympathy lifts the subject to a higher stage beyond the lonely imprisonment of searching to satisfy his own urges. The person is no longer responding simply to the sexual "charge" of the body as a source of pleasure; the person is attuned to "the whole person of the [opposite] sex, the whole man or woman" (*LR*, 110). If sensuality is like the water in the soil that surrounds a vine, sympathy is like the juice of the grape that grows on it. The water (sensuality) is good in itself, but if it remains in the soil, it will stagnate and become useless. It can be fruitful only if it is absorbed by the plant, which raises the water beyond itself and transforms it into the tasty, richly colored juice of the grape (sympathy).

Just as the water needs to be transformed into the juice of the grape, sensuality needs to be integrated into sentiment through the cultivation of sympathy. Nevertheless, sympathy is only a provisional fulfillment of sensuality, not the final stop on our journey toward the fullness of love. Sentiment, even when it flowers in sympathy, does not yet value the other person in his or her full depth, but focuses instead on the attraction emanating from the beloved as male or female. Consequently, we can't rely on sympathy alone to teach us to love, just as we can't light a road in the dark with fireworks or build a house on quicksand. Lovers who "as soon as sympathy breaks down . . . feel that love has also come to an end" (*LR*, 90) were never mature enough for love in the first place.

Like sensuality, sentiments alone are blind to the value of the person. Think of how lovers tend to idealize their beloved. Their incapacity to see a loved one's defects is symptomatic of a deeper and much more dangerous blindness. Instead of loving the actual flesh-and-blood person before them, they love an idealized object whose value they gauge exclusively by their own subjective reactions to it. Such idealization does not exalt the beloved but actually degrades his or her true dignity, for it overlooks the real person, who is much more than the feelings that he or she awakens in us.

If love were simply a matter of feelings, lovers would ultimately remain divided from each other, in spite of all their efforts and protests to the contrary. Sentiment, like sensuality, also points beyond itself to a higher level of love that mere feelings cannot attain. Sentiment points to affirmation of the value of the person, but by itself it is incapable of appreciating this value, because this level of relationship transcends the world of feelings. The fullness of love requires what Karol Wojtyla calls the *"affirmation of the person,"* which, as we will now see, involves a shift to a higher dimension of reality beyond the reach of mere feeling.

Affirming the Person

The attraction to another person based on feelings needs to mature into a yes to the value of the person him- or herself. Take, for example, Adam's love for Eve. This love needs to ripen into an affirmation of the worth that she possesses as a person independently of how he happens to feel about her. True love is not based alone on Eve's good qualities or on the splendid feelings she arouses in Adam, but on the marvelous fact that she simply *is* the particular person she is. To love truly is to keep on loving even on the bad days when sadness, annoyance, or ill humor temporarily drive those happier emotions out of our minds.

The affirmation of the person incorporates sensuality and sentiment, while at the same time going deeper than either of them can delve. It penetrates to the bedrock that alone is solid enough to support a stable relationship of love with another person. So long as we remain within the confines of mere sentiment, we can't say yes without reserve, because we are still at the mercy of the fluctuation of feelings whose very nature is to come and go. Only when love has discovered and affirmed the person for what he or she is can the lover say yes forever.

To remain within the realm of feeling is to be stuck in yourself, to be a prisoner of your perceptions of, and reactions to, the world. If we submit ourselves to sentiment as our absolute rule, we will fall into what Karol Wojtyla calls the "egoism of the feelings." By contrast, when we finally break through to the affirmation of another person for his or her own sake, when we finally learn to accept the beloved's dignity as someone other than ourselves, our existence is enriched by the new presence we thereby let into our inner world.

We have seen how even feelings open the prospect of a "we" by enabling us to share a common world with another. The affirmation of the value of the beloved cements this sharing on a whole new level of stability. Lovers who attain this new level share not only their feelings, but also their whole depth as persons. Firmly rooted in this mutual affirmation, man and woman are ready to join whole lives with each other in marriage. The highest stage of love, then, is what Karol Wojtyla calls "betrothed love," in which we find ourselves by giving ourselves to another. Betrothed love is doubly paradoxical: firstly in that it is possible to step outside one's own "I" in this way, and secondly in that the "I" far from being destroyed or impaired as a result is enlarged and enriched—of course in a super-physical, a moral sense. The Gospel stresses this very clearly and unambiguously—"would lose—shall find again," "would save—shall lose." (*LR*, 97)

Benedict XVI describes the ascent of love we've just traced with the help of the Song of Songs, which employs two Hebrew words to describe love:

> First there is the word *dodim*, a plural form suggesting a love that is still insecure, indeterminate and searching. This comes to be replaced by the word *ahabà*, which . . . becomes the typical expression for the biblical notion of love. Love now becomes concern and care for the other. No longer is it self-seeking, a sinking in the intoxication of happiness; instead it seeks the good of the beloved: it becomes renunciation and it is ready, and even willing, for sacrifice. (*DCE*, 6)

Needless to say, loving another person for his or her own sake doesn't suppress sensuality and sentiment. These other dimensions of love remain necessary aids to discovering and nurturing genuine love for another person. They help us to discover the value of the person, although they must also be integrated into, and point toward, this dignity: "So in every situation in which we experience the sexual value of a person, love demands integration, meaning the incorporation of that value in the value of the person, or indeed its subordination to the value of the person" (*LR*, 123).

Let's return to our example of the vine. Sensuality, we said, is like the water that the plant absorbs through its roots and transforms into the juice of the grapes. But the grapes themselves can be transformed in their turn into wine. Wine stands for the joy of the wedding feast that crowns betrothed love.

The example of the vine underscores the indispensable role all three dimensions—sensuality, sentiment, and affirmation—play in building up love. The wine (the affirmation of the person) contains the juice of the grape (sentiment), which in turn contains the water taken up from the soil (sensuality). Reducing love to feelings alone isolates us in a prison of egoism, yet leaving feelings out of account is almost as bad, for according to John Paul it deprives our love of warmth and undermines our capacity for real union with another person:

> There is, therefore, a need for sympathy to ripen into friendship and this process normally demands time and reflection . . . On the other hand, it is also necessary to supplement friendship with sympathy, without which it will remain cold and incommunicable. This process is possible, for although sympathy is born in human beings spontaneously and persists irrationally, it gravitates in the direction of friendship, it has a tendency to become friendship. This is a direct consequence of the structure of the inner self of a person, in which only things fully justified by free will and belief acquire full value. (*LR*, 92)[8]

Together Toward God

To love another person is to affirm this person for his or her own sake. If we look at this affirmation more closely, though, it turns out to be something of a mystery. On the one hand, the beloved is a finite human being as we are. On the other hand, affirming the beloved for his or her own sake means ascribing an absolute value to a human person. How is it possible to pronounce an infinite yes to a finite being?

> How can it be done, Teresa,
> for you to stay in Andrew forever?
> How can it be done, Andrew,
> for you to stay in Teresa forever
> since man will not endure in man
> and man will not suffice? (*JS*, 292)

The Jeweler's question to Teresa and Andrew seems to leave us with a choice between one of two equally unacceptable options: Either we force the beloved into the role of an absolute, thereby cruelly subjecting him or her to an infinite demand no mere human being could ever live up to, or else we affirm the beloved only conditionally, thereby refusing him or her the absolute yes that true love requires. Vatican II suggests a way out of this dilemma in a passage from *Gaudium et Spes* that underscores man's special dignity as the only creature on earth that God has loved for its own sake (*GS*, 24). The dignity of the person is indeed absolute, Vatican II is telling us, but this dignity is itself based on the absolute Source of all dignity: God. Human dignity resolves the dilemma we've been struggling with here as follows: Since the beloved is God's image, we can affirm him or her with an absolute yes; on the other hand, since our yes derives its force from the beloved's relation to God, that affirmation does not turn the beloved into an idol but frees him or her from the crushing load of a false absolutization that injures the beloved's dignity instead of exalting it.

A corollary of what we've just said is that we have no business ex-pecting another person to bear the whole burden of making us happy. Love's gravitational pull does not come to its final rest in our fellow creatures, but only in God. As Pope Benedict says, "[l]ove is indeed ecstasy, not in the sense of a moment of intoxication, but rather as a journey, an ongoing exodus out of the closed inward-looking self to-wards its liberation through self-giving, and thus towards authentic self-discovery and indeed the discovery of God" (*DCE*, 6).

It would be totally mistaken to conclude from the pope's words, however, that we need to turn away from our fellow human beings in order to turn toward God. For it is precisely *in* other persons, and in our *relationship* to them, that we find the presence of God. We don't make our journey to God away from other persons, then, but together with them. We will develop this point further in our next chapter.

A related implication of the foregoing is that all the aspects of personal existence we have considered thus far (sensuality, feelings, the affirmation of the person) direct us toward the ultimate goal of life, which is communion with God. We need not, in fact, we *should* not, ignore the lower dimensions of love, or despise our desires and feelings. Rather than rejecting them, we need to integrate them into love's basic movement toward God. When all of our affectivity, all of our bodily desires, are integrated into our affirmation of the value of the person, our sensuality and feelings aren't left behind but become part of our journey to the Absolute. It's precisely because it exists to be incorporated into such a journey that sexuality seems to promise an almost divine ecstasy of fulfillment.

Saint Augustine, then, was right when he called the affections the feet of our soul, by which we either walk toward God or away from him.[9] Karol Wojtyla makes a similar point in *Radiation of Fatherhood*. Feelings, Wojtyla says, need to be bathed in the light of the person and transfigured by the radiance of God's love:

> But what emerges on the wave of the heart
> should not develop haphazardly, leading into blind alleys.
> Every feeling, my child, must be permeated by light,
> so that one does not feel in darkness, but in the light, anew.
> (*RF*, 353)

FREEDOM IN LOVE

In the first chapter of this book, we accompanied Adam—who stands for all of us—as he responded to reality's surprising invitation to embark upon a quest for his own identity. In this second chapter, we've seen that man's encounter with love fulfills his quest for himself yet does not bring the journey to an end. Instead of diminishing wonder, love heightens it. In fact, love itself turns out to be the biggest surprise of all; it sheds a dazzling new light on the meaning of the original call man first heard in his initial encounter with reality. While chapter 1 presented man's existence as a call, a vocation (from the Latin *vocare*, "to call"), chapter 2 has fleshed out the nature of this call: Man is called to love.

The call to love resounding in man's body invites him to go out of himself and to build a world together with another. Adam and Eve's union begins in sensuality and feeling, but this initial experience is in turn a call to love, and the response to this call demands their free involvement. They must exercise their freedom to love by journeying from affective union (which consists in a mutual sharing of feelings) to the total communion of life based on their affirmation of each other as persons.

John Paul II used to say that God has given man his body as a task. We hope that the present chapter has clarified the nature of this task, which is to build up, and express, love for another person in and through the body. The accomplishment of this task is a shared work by means of which we "create" the beloved and are in turn "created" by him or her in love (we can speak of "creation" here because love fosters the other's growth into the fullness of God's creative intention for him or her). Love is reciprocal re-creation, the mutual bestowal of a name only lovers can utter. This mutuality is freedom's native air. For freedom isn't so much autonomy and independence as it is the capacity to express the union of love in the body and to foster the body's growth toward communion.

Human experience, then, springs from a call. But who is it that calls? On one level, of course, the origin of the call is another person of the opposite sex whose presence awakens love in us. But we need to take this initial answer to a deeper level. We have already seen that the dignity of the human person reveals the presence of God. It is God's voice that resounds in the call to love that our human beloved embodies. The work of the next chapter, to which we now turn, will be to discern the voice of the original Caller echoing in human love.

CHAPTER 3

THE NUPTIAL MYSTERY: FROM THE ORIGINAL GIFT TO THE GIFT OF SELF

OUR JOURNEY BEGAN WITH THE WONDER THAT ADAM experiences in his encounter with the world. We saw that this wonder reveals to him a hidden call and sets his restless heart on a quest to understand the meaning of his life and to grasp the origin and goal of his existence. As we saw in the previous chapter, the gift of Eve takes this quest to a new level: "This is bone of my bones and flesh of my flesh." Adam's act of naming Eve leads him deeper into his own identity. In naming her, he discovers his own name, too, as the wordplay in the Hebrew text of Genesis makes clear: "She will be called woman (*'iššāʰ*), because from man (*'iš*) she has been taken."

Although Adam's encounter with Eve is a decisive high point in his quest, it is not the end of his search. Instead of diminishing his wonder, the presence of Eve intensifies it: "This at last!" Of all the things that arouse wonder, love is the most wondrous. Eve's presence is not so much like a harbor for a storm-tossed ship as it is like the parting of the storm clouds to reveal a wider, more mysterious horizon toward which the ship continues its journey. As Teresa says just after Andrew has asked for her hand in the *Jeweler's Shop*:

I remember that Andrew did not turn his eyes to me at once,
but looked ahead for quite a while, as if gazing intently
at the road before us. (*JS*, 24)

A new experience of wonder always prepares a new stage of our
journey toward the Horizon of our existence, which is also the
Source from which all wonder ultimately comes.

If you want to find the source,
you have to go up, against the current.
Break through, search, don't yield,
you know it must be here somewhere.
Where are you? ... Source, where are you? (*RT*, 9)

This general rule is never truer than in the case of Adam's encounter with Eve, which ushers the two into a new world of wonder in
which both of them continue their journey toward the Source hand
in hand. In exploring this new stage of Adam's quest, John Paul II
develops what he calls a "hermeneutics of the gift," an interpretation
of our experience of reality in light of the gift that this reality is. But
what do we mean by "gift"? What does the idea of gift tell us about
our relationship to the Absolute? Source, what is your name?

ACKNOWLEDGING THE GIFT

Real wonder arises only in response to a gift. Only an act of generosity that we couldn't have engineered and that we cannot repay
suffices to awaken wonder in our hearts. For if we could engineer or
repay it, if it really did originate from us, it would be a mirror image

of what we already are or have. By the same logic, it would lack the element of surprise that is needed to inspire wonder in us. Let's apply this insight to Adam's encounter with Eve.

As he surveys the nonhuman creatures that populate the world around him, Adam might be forgiven for imagining that his unique dignity gave him an ability to measure their full value. But when Adam stands face-to-face with the woman, this impression vanishes in a flash. Instead, Adam is struck with wonder at a fellow person who, like him, can be measured only by the Absolute. In the encounter with Eve, Adam crosses a new threshold of wonder. Wonder has been given a name (see *RT*, 8).

Another way of putting this is that the creation of Eve engenders in Adam the first clear consciousness that reality is a gift flowing from the hand of Someone greater than he is. We say "Some*one*," rather than "some*thing*," because only persons can give gifts in the full sense of the word "give." "The concept of 'giving' cannot refer to nothing. It indicates the one who gives and the one who receives the gift, as well as the relation established between them" (*TOB*, 180).

As this passage makes clear, a gift establishes a relationship between persons; gift giving involves by definition a giver, a receiver, and the new relationship that the gift creates between them. By contrast, no lasting relationship is required when I make a purchase. Since a purchase mainly involves objects having such and such a price, if I deem them too expensive, poor in quality, or unsuitable to my needs, I can refuse to buy them without worrying about offending the seller. Just the opposite is true of receiving a gift: To refuse it means to hurt the person who wishes me to have it. What accounts for this striking difference between purchasing a product and receiving a gift?

An anecdote from the life of the German poet Rainer Maria

Rilke illustrates the creative possibilities of the gift. One day Rilke and a friend happened to pass a church where an old woman was begging at the gate. Rilke's companion offered her some change, and the poor woman, accustomed to the mechanical gestures of the passersby, took the money without even raising her eyes. Rilke, like a true poet, bought her a rose and presented it to her when the two friends passed by the church again later that day. The woman's response to Rilke's apparently useless offer was totally different from her reaction to the change proffered by his friend: She raised her eyes and smiled and was not seen at the gate of the church for a whole week afterward. When Rilke's friend asked him what she had lived on during that week, Rilke answered without missing a beat: She has lived on the rose.[1]

Rilke's rose was a unique and personal gift that touched the very dignity of the person who received it, reawakening her to life, whereas the change handed her mechanically by the passersby did not evoke any real human response in her soul.

It goes without saying, of course, that gift giving is a risky enterprise. Since a gift exists to be received, every act of giving necessarily entails the risk of being refused. Notice that the refusal of the intended gift is not the rejection of a mere object; it extends, in a certain sense, to the very person of the giver. Conversely, if the gift is accepted, a new relationship comes into being that enriches both giver and receiver. As Saint Irenaeus of Lyons said, "he who offers is himself glorified in what he does offer, if his gift be accepted."[2]

A gift is not just an object, but comes with it the person of the giver him- or herself. When we give a present, we are giving more than a piece of merchandise whose value can be measured by its market price. To give a gift is always, in one way or another, to give oneself. A gift establishes or strengthens a relationship that touches, in different degrees, the personal core of both giver and receiver. Ralph Waldo Emerson expressed it this way:

> The only gift is a portion of thyself. Thou must bleed for me. Therefore the poet brings his poem; the shepherd, his lamb; the farmer, corn; the miner, a gem; the sailor, coral and shells; the painter, his picture; the girl, a handkerchief of her own sewing. This is right and pleasing, for it restores society in so far to its primary basis, when a man's biography is conveyed in his gift.[3]

Emerson's words suggest that there is no gift giving without reciprocity. A gift does not need to be repaid, but it does need to be accepted. It's important to stress that the receiver is not degraded by accepting the gift with a thank-you. On the contrary, by gratefully acknowledging the gift, the receiver becomes a co-creative partner in the new relationship that the gift establishes. This reciprocity enriches both the one who gives and the one who receives. As John Paul II says: "giving and accepting the gift interpenetrate in such a way that the very act of giving becomes acceptance, and acceptance transforms itself into giving" (*TOB*, 196).

Let's sum up what we've seen so far about gift giving. A gift, we've said, can only be given for free. The reason the gift has to be gratis is not that it's "cheap." The point is that the gift has a kind of value that strictly speaking cannot be repaid. Why not? Because a gift expresses the unique worth of the person who gives it. What the giver seeks from the receiver, in fact, is not repayment, but a personal response. That's why the acceptance of the gift creates a relationship between giver and receiver, a relationship that enriches both of them at once. "Love," observes Saint Ignatius of Loyola in his *Spiritual Exercises*, "consists in a mutual sharing of goods, for example, the lover gives to the beloved, and shares with the beloved, what he possesses . . . and vice versa the beloved shares with the lover."[4] Saint John of the Cross sums up this creative power of the gift when he writes: "Where there is no love, put love and there you will draw out love."[5]

THE ORIGINAL GIVER

Let's return to the story of Adam and Eve, which confirms what we have been saying about the gift. For it is Eve *herself* who elicits Adam's wonder and delight—and not primarily any *thing* that she might give to, or do for, him. Her very person is a gift to him. The acknowledgment that the beloved him- or herself is a gift is the heart of every true love. The English poet Elizabeth Barrett Browning reminds us that what we love about the beloved isn't this or that quality he or she may *have*, but the very person he or she *is*:

> Do not say
> "I love her for her smile—her look—her way
> Of speaking gently,—for a trick of thought
> That falls in well with mine, and certes brought
> A sense of pleasant ease on such a day"—
> For these things in themselves, Beloved, may
> Be changed, or change for thee,—and love, so wrought,
> May be unwrought so.[6]

Real love doesn't stop with the "gentle voice" or the "sense of pleasant ease." It goes further to acknowledge the deeper reality that such things betoken. That is, it receives the very existence of the beloved as a gift. Adam revels in the goodness of Eve's very existence, just as she revels in the goodness of his; it is as if they said to each other: "It is good that you exist and that we exist together." It's only when lovers recognize this depth dimension in each other that their love becomes hardy enough to outlast changes in their feelings or alterations in their qualities and attributes.

What genuine lovers care about most is not simply whether the beloved can give him- or herself freely to them in return. True lovers who have attained the maturity of love are able to recognize that the beloved him- or herself is a gift, prior to any of his or her actions. In short, true love is a response to the very fact that the beloved's existence is itself already a gift.

Adam and Eve know deep in their bones that the call of love precedes anything that they could do to earn or produce it. They sense that they have been entrusted to each other even before they have a chance to choose whether they will belong to each other or not. Their very masculinity and femininity bring this situation home to them with all desirable clarity—not as a cruel chain that oppresses their freedom, of course, but as a gift that makes freedom possible and sets it on the road to its true fulfillment.

But who is it that first gives Adam and Eve to each other? Who ultimately entrusts Adam with the existence of Eve and Eve with the existence of Adam? Who calls Adam and Eve to accept each other as a gift that awakens in each a self-gift in response? To whom is Adam speaking when he exclaims: "This at last is bone of my bones"?

Adam's quest begins when he awakens to the world in a spirit of wonder. This encounter with the world invites him to set out on a journey toward the transcendent Absolute: "Source, where are you?" Adam begins to live out his quest for the Absolute in the body, which is his "organ" for receiving the world and participating in it, for tilling the soil and naming the animals (to use the biblical imagery).

Nevertheless, Adam's encounter with Eve takes his search to a whole new level. What his body opens him, indeed *calls* him, to receive is no longer just the world that has been entrusted to his stewardship, but another person who, like him, can be measured only by the Absolute.

So who first gives Adam and Eve to each other? The answer is God: "In the mystery of creation, man and woman were in a particular way 'given' to one another by the Creator" (*TOB*, 200). God is the original Giver who entrusts Eve to Adam and invites him to give himself to her (and vice versa):

> [T]he woman, who in the mystery of creation "is given" by the Creator to the man, is "welcomed" or accepted by him as a gift . . . At the same time, the acceptance of the woman by the man and the very way of accepting her become, as it were, a first gift in such a way that the woman, in giving herself . . . at the same time "discovers herself," thanks to the fact that she has been accepted and welcomed and thanks to the way in which she has been received by the man. (*TOB*, 196)

John Paul II often cited the affirmation in *Gaudium et Spes* that "man, who is the only creature on earth which God willed for itself, cannot fully find himself except through a sincere gift of himself" (*GS*, 24). According to the pope, this text of Vatican II implies that Adam can accept Eve only if he recognizes that she is a gift coming from the hands of the same original Giver who is at the origin of his, Adam's, very being. As Adam exclaims in *The Jeweler's Shop*: "Ah, Anna, how am I to prove to you that on the other side of all those loves which fill our lives—there is Love!" (*JS*, 64). The original Giver is represented in the play by the character of the Jeweler, who in one scene asks Anna and Stefan, a couple living in a marriage fraught with uncertainty and mistrust: "What are you building, children? What cohesion are these feelings of yours going to have beyond the Jeweler's message, of which the vertical axis cuts across every marriage in this world?" (*JS*, 81). The Jeweler then adds: "The thing is that love carries people away like an *absolute*, although it lacks absolute dimensions. But acting under an illusion, they do not try to connect that love with the Love that has such a dimension. They do not even feel the need, blinded as they are" (*JS*, 88).

In encountering each other, Adam and Eve encounter "the Love that has the dimension of the Absolute." Our next topic is the bodily nature of man's and woman's encounter with each other and, in each other, with God.

THE BODY:
A TESTAMENT TO THE ORIGINAL GIFT

Let's pause for a moment to retrace the steps we've taken up till now. First of all, we've seen that the body is the bearer of a revelation; it opens a common world for us to share with another person of the opposite sex. The body discloses this new horizon to us, moreover, by calling us to mutual self-giving. Indeed, this call to reciprocal self-giving is inscribed in the body's very masculinity and femininity by the original Giver. Having made this discovery, we are now ready to consider what this call tells us about the significance of the human body.

John Paul II defines the call inscribed in the masculinity and femininity of the body as its "nuptial meaning." The adjective "nuptial," which evokes the idea of marriage, underscores that the body is made to express love. The body is "nuptial" because it exists to enable Adam to give himself to Eve and to receive her as a gift (and vice versa). For John Paul, however, the nuptial meaning of the body isn't simply "horizontal"; it relates man and woman not merely to each other but also "vertically" to the original Giver who is the Source from whom they receive both themselves and each other as a gift:

> This is *the body*: *a witness* to creation as a fundamental gift, and therefore a *witness to Love as the source from which this same giving springs*. Masculinity-femininity . . . is the original sign of a creative donation and at the same time the sign of a gift that man, male-female, becomes aware of as a gift lived so to speak in an original way. (*TOB*, 183)

The "nuptial meaning" of the body is thus an invitation, written into our very corporeality, to recognize that everything we have is a gift, beginning with our own selves and our very existence. The "nuptiality" of the body thus establishes a relationship with the Absolute; it reveals God as a Father who gives us life and surrounds us with his care. By the same token, our first task—or, rather, privilege—in life is to accept the original gift of our own existence. Ersilio Cardinal Tonini relates an anecdote that beautifully illustrates this privilege: "Up till now," his mother once told him as a child, "I have received you, every day of my life, as a gift of God. Now it is your turn to do the same: receive yourself every day as God's gift."[7]

What we've said amounts to another way of describing original solitude—the special dignity that makes man superior to the animals. Only human beings can appreciate their existence as a gift. Seen in the light of "nuptiality," original solitude turns out to be man's distinctive capacity to understand the witness of his own body, which teaches him the giftedness of his very existence. Using the words of Saint Irenaeus, we could say that original solitude is the experience that "in the beginning...God formed Adam...that He might have someone upon whom to confer His benefits."[8]

Normally, we tend to measure our own body by the objects in the world around us.[9] John Paul II's appreciation of the dignity of the human body calls us to revolutionize our thinking: Instead of measuring the meaning of our body by the objects around us, we must learn to measure the objects around us by the "nuptial meaning" of our body. This does not mean, of course, that we are entitled to treat nature as a mere object. On the contrary, since all of creation is a gift, there is actually no such thing as a "mere" object, and man's dominion over the earth must be founded on a recognition that all of reality comes from the Creator's love. Original solitude, or the awareness that we ourselves are the greatest gift of all, does not rule out appreciation of the gift of creation, but (logically speaking) it is the only possible foundation on which such appreciation can be built.

Just as our wonder at the sight of lofty mountain peaks or the vast expanse of the sea is rooted in our at least dim or inchoate awareness that we ourselves are the greatest gift of all, Eve's presence opens Adam's eyes to a new way of looking at the rest of the world. It is not true that love is blind, as the saying goes. Instead, paraphrasing Saint Augustine, we could say that "love has its own eyes." The eyes of love, the eyes of a heart that sees (see *DCE*, 31), perceive every object we touch and every moment we live as a gift.

In Thornton Wilder's play *Our Town*, Emily, a young woman who has just passed away, is given the chance to relive one day of her former life on earth. Emily is, of course, eager to enjoy every minute at her disposal, but, to her dismay, her relatives, friends, and neighbors are simply too caught up in their hectic busyness to share her joy in being alive. When Emily wonders aloud whether anyone realizes how precious life is, her mother-in-law answers that only the poets and the saints sometimes do.[10] Fortunately, no one is completely excluded from this prerogative of the poets and saints. Adam and Eve enjoyed it to the full in Eden, and the same gift is still granted in some way to every child who comes into the world. Everyone is a potential poet and saint, and everyone possesses an inborn capacity to experience his or her living body as a gift that inaugurates a relationship with the original Giver.

FROM THE ORIGINAL GIFT
TO THE GIFT OF SELF

God is the Source of the gift that we are to ourselves. But what about the mutual self-giving we talked about earlier in this chapter? What about love? One of the questions Benedict XVI seeks to answer in his first encyclical, *Deus Caritas Est*, is precisely whether it's actually possible to love, and to give oneself to, another person. The pope answers this question in the affirmative, but then adds that we can love one another only because we have been loved first by God. We can become a spring of love only if we have first drunk from love's divine Source:[11] "He has loved us first and he continues to do so; we too, then, can respond with love. God does not demand of us a feeling which we ourselves are incapable of producing. He loves us, he makes us see and experience his love, and since he has 'loved us first,' love can also blossom as a response within us" (*DCE*, 17).

The fact that God loves us first explains how the Bible can reasonably command our love in response. Our intuition tells us that nobody can *command* us to love, and that love commanded would no longer be true love. How, then, can Jesus lay down love of God and neighbor as *the* commandment par excellence? The Bible answers this question by putting the commandments in the context of a gift that precedes them: "I am the LORD your God, who brought you out of the land of Egypt" (Exod. 20:2). The commandment of love makes sense, in other words, only in terms of the prior gift embodied in God's actions on behalf of his people. Consequently, this commandment is not a harsh and unreasonable order, but the inner law of the gift itself. The commandment to love is a commandment to be grateful, that is, to do justice to the gift with which we have been entrusted from the beginning.

In the final act of *The Jeweler's Shop*, Teresa's son Christopher and Anna's daughter Monica, though recently engaged, have not yet discovered that their relationship is rooted in a love that is even greater still. Karol Wojtyla metaphorically describes the young couple's immaturity as a failure to appreciate the artistry the Jeweler displays in fashioning their wedding rings. In the words of Monica: "He did nothing to fascinate us . . . he simply measured, first, the circumference of our fingers, then of the rings, as an ordinary craftsman would. There was no artistry in it even. He did not bring us closer to anything. All the beauty remained in our own feeling" (*JS*, 80). Unlike Christopher and Monica, Christopher's mother, Teresa, knows from experience that the depth and maturity of true love hinges on the couple's recognition of the Jeweler's skill in forging the rings that symbolize their destiny as human beings:

> I must go up to them and say this: "My children, nothing has ceased to be, man must return to the place from which his existence grows"—and how strongly he desires it to grow through

love. And I know that the old jeweler . . . gave you the same look, as if he were sounding your hearts and defining through those rings a new level of existence. (*JS*, 79)

This scene from *The Jeweler's Shop* illustrates the truth that love is a much deeper affair than many lovers realize, for it calls on them to receive each other as God's gift and in so doing to embark upon the adventure of a concrete relationship with the Giver himself. God reveals his love for the first man and woman by entrusting each of them with the other as a precious gift in whom his divine Love delights. The love Adam and Eve share wouldn't be fully human outside the "dimension of the Absolute." They enjoy all the delight of real love only because their relationship to each other is at the same time a relationship to God. Human lovers love in truth only when they receive themselves from, and give themselves to, God in the very act of receiving themselves from, and giving themselves to, each other. As the philosopher Jean Guitton says:

> We only love truly if we love in a sphere which is superior to us, in a unity more lofty and more fulfilled, in a plenary term which assures the union of the [two lovers]. Just as respiration supposes an atmosphere, so love calls for an *erosphere* . . . [T]he true and real term which unites the loves, which establishes them . . . is that which men have named God.[12]

MOTHERHOOD AND FATHERHOOD

Couples can love each other only to the extent that they let the Creator "define a new level of existence" that places their love in the context of the Absolute. Yet the presence of the original Giver in Adam and Eve's mutual love doesn't just transport them both across a new threshold of wonder; it also completes this wonder in the mystery of fruitfulness. The Bible recounts that "Adam knew Eve his wife" (Gen. 4:1). The verb *to know* underscores that the first couple discover their identity through their conjugal union. But it does something more as well: It connects this disclosure with the physical fruitfulness in which the couple cement their union by sharing in God's act of engendering new life. "Procreation is rooted in creation, and every time it reproduces in some way its mystery" (*TOB*, 169). Eve recognizes the divine root of her fruitfulness after the birth of her first child: "I have gotten a man," she exclaims, "with the help of the LORD" (Gen. 4:1). Here is John Paul II glossing this biblical text:

> And when they become "one flesh"
> —that wondrous union—
> on the horizon there appears the mystery of fatherhood and
>   motherhood.
> They return to the source of life within them
> —They return to the beginning.
> —Adam knew his wife
> and she conceived and gave birth.
> They know that they have crossed the threshold
> of the greatest responsibility! (*RT*, 21)

Adam and Eve cross the threshold of wonder in their conjugal union (*RT*, 8), but the fecundity of their union is in turn the first step toward a new threshold, that of responsibility. Fruitfulness is the culmination of active *response* to the wonderment that seizes us when we receive one another as God's gift. For the same reason, "procreation" is a more suitable description of fecundity than "reproduction," because it underscores man's participation in the work of creation that the very Source of life entrusts to him through the conjugal act. "Procreation" has the added advantage of highlighting the difference between the production of objects and the communication of life to beings possessed of unique dignity as unrepeatable, irreplaceable persons whose existence is willed by God for its own sake.

It's worth noting here how the presence of divine love within conjugal union enriches our understanding of freedom. God's presence in spousal love brings home to us that freedom cannot exist apart from grateful recognition of the original gift; freedom flourishes only when we realize that the whole of our existence is a free gift. Recall the scene in Dante's *Purgatorio* when nightfall temporarily suspends the poet's ascent of Mount Purgatory. To continue the path up the mountainside is to gain freedom, but after dark descends one can only walk either around the mountain or down it, but not up it. The upward path requires daylight, which symbolizes the divine love that makes freedom possible. It's only in the liberating light of God's love that we can outgrow the narrow confines of the self and climb the mountain of love for God and neighbor toward the crown that awaits us at its summit.[13]

MASCULINITY AND FEMININITY: SIGNPOSTS TO THE SOURCE OF LOVE

The discovery of the ground on which love is built, and of the fruit this ground yields, helps us appreciate the meaning of masculinity and femininity in a new light. We can gauge just how new this light is if we recall for a moment the ancient myth of the Androgyne that the Greek philosopher Plato puts in the mouth of one of the characters in his dialogue *The Symposium*. This myth explains the origin of the sexes as a punishment: Whereas man was originally an asexual unit perfectly complete in itself, the gods divided him into two parts (male and female), which, so the tale concludes, have been longing to recover their lost unity ever since. It goes without saying that John Paul II's account of the Christian understanding of the sexes couldn't be more different. The pope knows, of course, that each sex refers to the other and can be understood only in light of the other. But he vigorously distinguishes this complementarity from the idea that man and woman are just incomplete "parts" of humanity, like the two halves of the single "whole" divided by the avenging gods in the myth of the Androgyne. John Paul insists that man and woman are *both* whole, even though each sex embodies this wholeness in a different form. It's important to add that this difference between male and female perdures even in their union. While each of the sexes is whole, both are called beyond themselves by and to the other.

We can illustrate the complementarity between man and woman with an image drawn from the world of music. Imagine that a symphony conductor calls upon his two most gifted violinists to perform a duet at the next concert. The two musicians will have to practice blending their instruments in harmonious counterpoint, each needing the other in order to express the complete piece as intended by the composer. Note, however, that this need is just the opposite of want of skill. The two violinists are not incompetent half musicians using each other to cover up the defects in their respective performances. Rather they are two consummate artists called upon to display their respective individual skill precisely within the context of a duet in which each player's role is inseparable from that of the other. It goes without saying that the two musicians can rise to the occasion, and excel in their joint performance, only if they are both open to being inspired by the same transcendent beauty shining through the piece the conductor calls upon them to play.

This example suggests that sexuality, like a score for two violins, is a pattern. This pattern gives the lovers' lives a relationship whose structure weaves together both harmony and counterpoint. At the same time, the music of relationship springs from a common inspiration; indeed, it bubbles up from the divine source of existence itself. The relationship between man and woman makes no sense unless both of them derive their identity from their relationship to the Creator. Masculinity and femininity are paths to the discovery of our identity in the encounter with God. They are, according to John Paul II, two incarnations of the same original solitude before God and the world:

> The knowledge of man passes through masculinity and femininity, which are, as it were, two "incarnations" of the same metaphysical solitude before God and the world—two reciprocally completing ways of "being a body" and at the same time of being human—as two complementary dimensions of self-knowledge and self-determination and, at the same time, two complementary ways of being conscious of the meaning of the body. Thus, as Genesis 2:23 already shows, femininity in some way finds itself before masculinity, while masculinity confirms itself through femininity. (*TOB*, 166)[14]

Because masculinity and femininity are the two basic ways of being open to God, to other human beings, and to the world, lovers who try to create a universe of their own from which everyone else is excluded do not exalt love but actually distort its true nature. The relationship between Adam and Eve stands in the larger context of their relationship with the Absolute, which in turn opens their union to the rest of the world. By the same token, masculinity and femininity tend by their very nature to participate in the Source of love through fatherhood and motherhood. We will have the occasion to return to paternity and maternity later in this book. For the time being, it suffices to bear in mind that the call to love comes not only from our human beloved but from the Source of Love who invites us to enter into greater communion with him through our love for our human beloved. By building up their relationship with one another, Adam and Eve enter into relationship with God. Perhaps we could even say that together they become his image. The face of God is most fully reflected in the communion uniting man and woman in a shared journey of love.

CHAPTER 4

THE COMMUNION OF PERSONS AS AN IMAGE OF THE TRINITY

ADAM AND EVE'S JOURNEY HAS TAKEN AN UNEXPECTED turn. At first they thought they were the ones searching for the Source, but now they realize that all along it was the Source who was searching for an opportunity to reveal himself to them both as a Giver and as a Father. Adam and Eve finally realize that their mutual love is an invitation to enter into a covenant with God, who has entrusted them to each other's care. In *The Jeweler's Shop*, Teresa and Andrew recount how this same realization dawned on them in the presence of the Jeweler:

> Our whole existence stood before Him. His eyes were flashing signals that we were not able to receive fully just then, as once we had been unable to receive fully the signals in the mountains—and yet they reached to our inner hearts. And somehow we went into their direction, and they covered the fabric of our lives. (*JS*, 43)

Later in the play, Teresa and Andrew are drawn by the Jeweler's "signals" to behold their reflection in his shop window (*JS*, 41–42).

As they contemplate their faces in the glass, they discover that, like Adam and Eve, they, too, are an image of God: "God created man in his own image, in the image of God he created him; male and female he created them" (Gen. 1:27).

"The Beginning and the End are invisible," says John Paul II in his *Roman Triptych*. But between the invisible beginning and end there runs a visible thread. This thread is the image of God that is unfurled in man's journey of love. But what is the "image of God" actually an image *of*? How can the Source be reflected in human love? How can man and woman partake in the Source? These are the questions that will engage our attention in the present chapter.

THE IMAGE OF A SON

Karol Wojtyla's play *Our God's Brother*, which we cited briefly in an earlier chapter, is a helpful introduction to the topic of the divine image in man. The play tells the story of Adam Chmielowski, a painter who gives up his art in order to follow Christ in the poor. Note that "Adam" isn't just a character in *Our God's Brother*; he is also a symbol of Everyman who represents our common human journey.

The motor driving the action of the play is Adam's restless search for the perfect image of beauty. As Adam pursues his quest, he has to struggle with an alien voice echoing in his heart. This voice, called "The Other" in the play, constantly whispers in Adam's ear: "Your special dignity is your intelligence" (see *OGB*, 201–5). "The Other," then, represents an autonomous intelligence that deems that man can achieve happiness on his own. Such an intelligence scorns any offer of outside help to reach happiness, an offer it despises as an affront to human dignity.

As the play progresses Adam eventually learns to counter the Other's logic of absolute autonomy with a deeper logic of image and likeness. At the sight of a poor man "leaning limply against a lamppost," Adam says, "There is something more in him than just a beggar leaning against a lamppost . . . There is an image . . . image and likeness." Adam then explains what this image and likeness consists in: "Ah, wait—likeness and image. You see—he is a child; he is a son. I too" (*OGB*, 204–5).

Adam's words "he is a child; he is a son" identify the "image" as a relation between father and son, or, in technical terms, as a relation of "filiation" (meaning "sonship," from the Latin word for "son," *filius*). This definition of the image in terms of sonship suggests another crucially important point: Man's special dignity does not derive from the possession of some supposedly pure and autonomous intelligence; it is based on sonly or filial relation to a Father who has brought him into existence and calls him to a life of communion and friendship. How, then, does this interpretation of the divine image in man square with the Bible?

The first chapter of Genesis teaches, as we know, that man is created in the image and likeness of God (Gen. 1:26–27); in what follows, we'll often use the Latin name for this divine image: *imago Dei*. Now, some Scripture scholars connect the *imago Dei* with man's task of exercising "dominion" over the earth through world-transforming work. Wojtyla agrees with this interpretation up to a point. Nevertheless, he qualifies his agreement in a subtle but profound way by placing the task of dominion in a larger context.

Wojtyla agrees, of course, that dominion over the earth is a *consequence* of man's special status as God's image, but he argues that the *essence* of the *imago Dei* is more than this function of representing divine authority on earth. Put another way, Wojtyla grants that God calls man to stewardship over creation, but he insists that the steward's role follows from, and depends on, an even more fundamental call to a special covenant relationship with the Creator himself. For Wojtyla, then, the most important truth about man is not that he rules over the earth, but that he is a partner of the Absolute;[1] this primordial relationship with God defines Adam's superiority to the rest of creation, not vice versa. Dominion, to repeat, is the first *consequence* of the *imago Dei*, not its *essence.*

The *imago Dei* is bound up with man's original solitude, which, recall, we defined as the distinctive human capacity to answer the Word of God that has called him into being. In *Our God's Brother*, as we have just seen, Adam connects man's status as the *imago Dei* with his call to become a son or daughter of God. This connection has a sound biblical basis. Isaiah, for example, compares God in the same breath to a potter who molds the clay (image) and to a father and mother who beget and bear children (sonship): "Woe to him who strives with his Maker . . . Dare the clay say to him who fashions it, 'What are you making'? . . . Woe to him who says to a father, 'What are you begetting?' or to a woman, 'With what are you in travail?' " (Isa. 45:9–10). Genesis completes Isaiah's thought by stressing that Adam and Eve transmit the *imago Dei* to their offspring through sexual generation (Gen. 5:3), which is another way of saying that human parenthood is a reflection of God's Fatherhood itself. It's no wonder, then, that John Paul II uses the idea of filiation to illustrate Adam and Eve's experience that they are a gift, both in themselves and for each other:

This consistent giving, which goes back to the deep roots of consciousness and the subconscious and to the final levels of the subjective existence of both man and woman and which is reflected in their reciprocal "experience of the body," bears witness to [the first man's] rootedness in Love ... In biblical language, that is, in the language of revelation, the qualification "first" means precisely "of God," "Adam, son of God" [Luke 3:38] ... In his time, Christ was to be a witness to this irreversible love of the Creator and Father, which had already expressed itself in the mystery of creation. (*TOB*, 190–91)

John Paul II's connection of original solitude with the idea of sonship clearly rules out any interpretation of the former as some sort of lonely isolation. Being an expression of the *imago Dei*, original solitude is actually just the opposite: It is a relationship with the very ground and foundation of life itself. Original solitude is openness to the Absolute; it is the joyful privilege of standing face-to-face with the original Giver who created the universe. In their original solitude, Adam and Eve come to know by experience that God, as Saint Athanasius says, "is good—or rather, of all goodness He is Fountainhead."[2]

The filiation theme sheds light on man's freedom. The Bible connects freedom with *sonship*, rather than with, say, the autonomous liberty of the isolated individual we tend to exalt today. Indeed, the ancients in general linked freedom to membership in the household as part of the family; slaves, while living physically among the family, were not members of it, but merely propertyless strangers. Saint Paul shared the ancient view that to be free was to be a son in the house of one's father. By the same token, he thought that the opposite of slavery was much more than just the absence of chains; freedom for Paul was the status of sonship thanks to which we enjoy membership in God's family (see Gal. 4:7). As Saint John puts it, "if the Son makes you free, you will be free indeed" (John 8:36).

THE IMAGE OF GOD IS A JOURNEY

The foregoing account of the *imago Dei* makes it clear that the divine image in man is much "thicker" than a reflection in a mirror or a picture of a king embossed on a coin. Such images are often quite similar to their originals, but they enjoy no living interaction with this original. Everything changes, though, when the image is a son begotten by a father. An image of this sort stands by definition in a living relationship with the original, from whom it is born and to whom it tends. Since the *imago Dei* clearly falls under this category of image, it isn't just a static representation; it is part of a dynamic process that reveals to us both our origin and our destiny.

The book of Genesis teaches that God made man in his "image and likeness." The Fathers of the Church set great store by the biblical text's distinction between image and likeness. In their view, this distinction served to bring out what they saw as the dynamic and relational character of the *imago Dei*. For the Fathers, the word "image" refers to the similarity between the human copy and the divine Original, a similarity that characterizes man from the first moment of his existence. "Likeness," on the other hand, is the dynamic dimension of the *imago Dei*, which man is called to perfect by growing ever closer to God in love. As the great theologian Saint Maximus Confessor puts it: "To the inherent goodness of the image is added the likeness acquired by the practice of virtue and the exercise of the will."[3]

For the Fathers, then, man is *born* as God's image, but he has to *complete* the *imago Dei* through his free yes to God. John Paul II shares in this vision. The divine image is seen as both a gift *and* a task: "This likeness is a quality of the personal being . . . and is also a call and a task" (see *MD*, 7). Insofar as it is a task, and not just a gift, the image of God takes time—indeed, a whole lifetime—to unfold its riches. The *imago Dei* is much more like a play that tells the story of our lives than it is like a snapshot that reflects only one moment in the story.

The life story of the *imago Dei* begins with the primordial human experience of childhood; receiving life from our parents allows us to realize that we are God's children. Because parents participate in God's own fatherhood, the revelation of the *imago Dei* begins in the family. Nevertheless, it is not enough just to be born or even to acknowledge our origin from God; we must also love in our turn, freely accepting God's gift of existence, and making that gift fruitful in our lives. Coming from another is only the initial phase of the image of God, the first stage on a lifelong journey to perfect likeness. So we still need to ask how the image, given in filiation, grows in likeness to the Original. How does the child return to the Source of love from whom he or she comes? As we will see, it is by maturing within a communion of persons that man attains the fullness of the divine image.

THE IMAGE IS REVEALED IN COMMUNION

There's a powerful scene in *Our God's Brother* that beautifully captures the failure of a pure intellectual approach to account for the relationship to others that is written into the fabric of the *imago Dei*. The voice of the Other, pushing the claims of autonomous intelligence, identifies man's dignity with his mental capabilities. But the Other has left something out of his argument: He's forgotten that these capabilities are gifts given by God *to enable man to know and love the Creator in communion with others.* Of course, Wojtyla isn't content simply to show how the Other completely misses the real heart of man's identity as an *imago Dei.* In a moving scene where Adam encounters a suffering tramp on the road, Wojtyla proposes a constructive alternative to the Other's misunderstanding of human dignity:

> *Adam:* Oh, do you see that man leaning against the lamppost?
> *The Other:* He does not attract my intelligence. He has ceased to
> be an issue for me. I can go past him.
> *Adam:* Oh, how much is missing in you, how much you miss!
>
> *[On the other side of Adam the even, unbroken darkness of the street expands. Adam has passed the place where the street lamp had cast the shadow. The Other is no more. Adam lifts the tramp, supporting him with his arm. He drags the man, who limps on his right leg.]*
>
> Come, my friend. You're not saying anything? Your hands...oh, you're freezing...You cannot walk...Well, come!...Come. You have saved me. (*OGB*, 205)

"You have saved me." Adam is saved because he has escaped the temptation to live in isolation under the sterile tyranny of mere intelligence. The tramp's reliance on Adam's help reminds Adam of his own dependence and opens his eyes to see that he, like the suffering man, is a son. Our filiation is revealed to us in our encounter with other human persons. This brings us back to Adam's encounter with Eve, which is a crucial moment in the revelation of sonship.

We saw in the previous chapter that Adam receives Eve as a gift

from God, just as Adam's giving of himself to Eve embodies God's
love for her. We saw, in other words, that the mutual love of the first
couple is enfolded within a relationship of love with God, the Source
of Life. This relationship, we can now add, is filial. By receiving each
other as God's gift and giving themselves to each other in return,
Adam and Eve accept their identity as children of God who walk
hand in hand back to the Father from whom they came.

We asked at the end of the previous section how man ratifies the
imago Dei and how he visibly embodies the Father's love in a life of
sonship. We now have the answer: He does so through the free, mutual self-giving of man and woman. As John Paul II explains in his
Letter to Women, God is revealed in the communion between man
and woman, for this communion images the love that God himself
is.[4] Benedict XVI makes the same point in one of his first speeches
as pope: "the human being," the pope affirms, "is created in the image of God, and God himself is love. It is therefore the vocation to
love that makes the human person an authentic image of God: Man
and woman come to resemble God to the extent that they become
loving people."[5]

Popes Benedict and John Paul II confront us with an astonishing
claim: Spouses love each other with a love that is greater than themselves, in fact, with the very love that brought them into existence
in the first place! The original gift of God's love permeates their relationship and endows them with the capacity to give themselves to
each other and, by so doing, to express their gratitude to the Giver
of their existence. To put the same idea less technically: *The love between spouses is nothing less than the visible presence of God's love in
the world.*

We noted earlier that the *imago Dei* is a dynamic relationship to the Father that we are called to live out in the adventure of sonship. We can add now that this very dynamism seeks active expression in the love that unites the spouses. The love of the child who knows he has received everything from the Father ripens by its very nature into spousal union. This union is in turn the royal road on which man and woman return together to God, fulfilling the "image" in the "likeness" that crowns it.

Nor is this all. Because the marital relation expresses a love greater than itself, it is fruitful. The visible sign of this fruitfulness is the child. "I have gotten a man," Eve exclaims, "with the help of the LORD" (Gen. 4:1). Adam, the son of God, who has received everything from the Father, shows his love for God by giving himself to Eve, the daughter of God, as her spouse (and vice versa). This gift is crowned by fecundity, which images the presence of the Father's love in human love down through the generations. The words Karol Wojtyla places in the mouth of Adam, the first man, in *Reflections on Fatherhood* underscore the continuity between filiality and fatherhood that we've been examining here: "To absorb the radiation of fatherhood means not only to become a father but, much more, to become a child (become a son). Being the father of many, many people, I must be a child: the more I am a father, the more I become a child" (*Ref Fath*, 368).

We noted earlier that, in order to understand the image of God, we need to watch it unfold over time. Man images God through a life story that bears witness to his invisible origin and end. We are who we are because Another has loved us into being and equipped us for mutual self-giving in fruitful spousal love. We derive our most basic identity as persons from our origin in Love, an origin that enables us to give ourselves in our turn to another in fruitful spousal love. It is this process—which John Paul II called "the genealogy of the person" in his *Letter to Families*—that transmits the image of God in time.[6]

The family contains a threefold pattern: In the family we discover that we are children and we are called to become spouses and parents.[7] This threefold temporal pattern shapes the person's growth into the divine image over time.[7] Let's briefly trace the unfolding of the divine image according to the threefold pattern inscribed in the body by the Creator.

THE *IMAGO DEI* IN THE BODY: "ORIGINAL NAKEDNESS"

It is tempting to suppose that the image of God resides exclusively in the human soul. After all, the soul is the seat of intelligence and free will, the two powers that raise man above the realm of material things. Given this natural tendency to identify the *imago Dei* with the soul, it may come as something of a shock to learn that John Paul II took a more inclusive view of the matter. The pope grants that the soul reflects the divine image, but he insists that the soul is not the only reflection of God in man. The image of God, while of course mirrored in the soul, also shines forth from the body as well.[8]

John Paul's extension of the *imago Dei* to the body is actually a revival of an ancient tradition going back to the earliest Fathers of the Church, who taught that "the Divine Creator formed" the flesh "with His own hands in the image of God."[9] But even if we welcome John Paul's restoration of the full bodiliness of the *imago Dei*, how are we supposed to make sense of the idea that the flesh images the divine? How can the body, which is material, contain the image of the invisible God, who by definition is a spirit that transcends matter?

The language of the body tells us that we are children (the body's filial meaning) who are called by that very fact to become spouses (the body's nuptial meaning) whose mutual love is a path to God. Since the body reflects God's own love, it cannot be foreign to the *imago Dei*. Of course, the body also exposes us to a vulnerability and dependence that at first sight seem to be anything but divine qualities. And yet, far from diminishing the body's participation in the image of God, its vulnerability is actually part and parcel of the dignity that comes with that imaging. God, we could say, reveals himself as love in the very weakness of the body. This claim may seem paradoxical, but it simply repeats the paradox of love itself. For love always makes space for the beloved, prompting the lover's humble acceptance of, and delight in, the beloved's glorious difference from himself. This isn't to deny, of course, that our intelligence and free will image God's power or his superiority over creation. The point is rather that these transcendent attributes reveal their true face only when they are filtered through the humility of the body. This humility of the body is a constant reminder that the Absolute is also a love who calls man to friendship with himself.

The ability to perceive the image of God imprinted on the human body is one of man's original experiences. Basing his discussion on Genesis 2:25 ("the man and his wife were both naked, and were not ashamed"), John Paul II calls this experience "original nakedness." Unlike some modern thinkers, however, John Paul argues that the absence of shame in the original state didn't proceed from some sort of psychological underdevelopment, as if Edenic humanity were still in a state of immaturity destined eventually to be left behind. On the contrary, original nakedness, like all of man's original experiences, contains a fullness that we have yet to grow into. If we have lost the ability to encounter one another without shame, it isn't because we have grown up but because we have fallen away from the foundation of our own existence and become separated from the true source of our maturity as human beings.

Put another way, original nakedness is the ability to read the language of the human body as a simultaneous expression of original solitude and original unity. If Adam and Eve were "naked and unashamed" before the Fall, it was because they knew how to discern the dignity of the human body and to recognize its difference from everything else in the visible world, both animate and inanimate. In a word, their original nakedness was nothing less than their clear-eyed realization that masculinity and femininity are made for a journey of communion toward the Source of the Gift.

Just as original nakedness has nothing to do with moral underdevelopment, it is also worlds removed from nudism. In fact, wearing clothes actually expresses original nakedness, because clothing underscores the special status of the body as an expression of the unique dignity of the human being. Living in harmony with original nakedness, then, doesn't mean going around in the nude but dressing in a way that conforms to one's dignity. The most fitting reflection of original nakedness is not nudity (or prudery), but a purity that reveals the mystery of our being without profaning it:

> "Male and female He created them."
> God bestowed on them a gift and a task.
> They accepted—in a human way—the mutual self-giving
> which is in Him.
> Both naked . . .
> they felt no shame, as long as the gift lasted—

Shame will come with sin,
yet the thrill remains. They live conscious of the gift,
without being able to call it by name.
But they live it, they are pure. (*RT*, 20)

John Paul II loved the frescoes of the Sistine Chapel, which for him attested to Michelangelo's sensitivity to the image of God being in the human body. John Paul knew, of course, that God is invisible: "The End," he writes in *Roman Triptych*, "is as invisible as the Beginning. The universe came forth from the Word, and returns to the Word" (*RT*, 22). Nevertheless, John Paul was convinced that the beginning and end of the world, though invisible in themselves, become visible to us in the human body as it journeys from the cradle to the grave. This insight sums up the pope's thinking about original nakedness, which is ultimately the human body's capacity to image God as Love. Accordingly, living in original nakedness simply means learning to discern the *imago Dei* with the eyes of the Creator, who always sees the body's connection with the whole person it expresses. Doing justice to original nakedness means reliving the original experience of the body that makes the mystery of God's love both visible and active:

He saw, and He found a trace of His Being—
He found reflection of Himself in all things visible.
The Eternal Word is, as it were, the threshold
beyond which we live and move and have our being...
   (*RT*, 17)

Pre-sacrament—existence itself as the outward sign of eternal
   Love. (*RT*, 21)

CHRIST'S NEW GIFT:
ENTERING INTO GOD'S COMMUNION

This chapter began with Teresa and Andrew, two characters from *The Jeweler's Shop*, as they catch sight of themselves reflected in the glass of the jeweler's display window. What we've learned so far is that the image they see gazing back at them is their "existence itself," the whole of which is "the outward sign of eternal Love." Indeed, Teresa and Andrew see the Jeweler's presence reflected in their love. Their love is embraced by the divine love itself: "[the jeweler's] shop window . . . became . . . a mirror reflecting us both—Teresa and myself . . . We were not only reflected but absorbed. I had an impression of being seen and recognized by someone hiding inside the shop window" (*JS*, 41–42).

But how can the love between Teresa and Andrew, their journey from the beginning toward the end, be taken up into the Source? How can spousal love be lifted up into the divine being himself? Only the "Good News" of Christianity provides us with a full answer to this question. For Christ's life and death reveal that God in himself is Love, that he is a communion of persons in which Father and Son are one in the Spirit who personifies divine love. An essential part of the Christian Gospel is therefore the message that God has a "space" in himself that is ample enough to embrace human love in all its grandeur.

We've already seen that man awakens within the family to the presence of God as a Father who endows him with the gift of existence. The revelation of God in Jesus Christ makes it finally clear that God doesn't begin to be a Father when he enters into relation to man. Rather paternity is a part of God's eternal being, and it was so long before man ever appeared on the scene. God has always been a Father, because from all eternity he has had a Son who receives everything from him. This Son is the eternal Child who opens a space in God for Adam and Eve to become children of the Father in their turn. Man is made to share in the filiation of the eternal Son, and so to make his eternal home in the very heart of God's being.

Now, God is not only present to Adam and Eve as the origin from whom they both come, but also as the goal to whom they journey. In fact, we've also seen that Adam and Eve experience God's love in the midst of their spousal exchange. In giving themselves to each other they not only accept the gift God has given them in entrusting each to the other; they also give themselves back to Him by loving each other. Thus, the spouses are united by a greatness (the presence of God's love in their love) that overcomes both of them. To this fundamental human experience Christ brings an unexpected fulfillment. He shows that this love that unites the man and the woman shares in the Holy Spirit, who eternally unites the Father and the Son in the communion of the Trinity. God's Love can introduce Adam and Eve into the very core of the mystery of his own being because this Love is not some *thing* other than God, but is the Holy Spirit himself, "the Person-gift" who empowers man to accept God's self-giving and initiates him into the Trinitarian communion.[10] Indeed, the Spirit's indwelling within human love "transfigures" the body into a transparent fulfillment of original nakedness. An incident from the life of the great Orthodox mystic Saint Seraphim of Sarov beautifully illustrates this transfiguration:

Father Seraphim took me very firmly by the shoulders and said: "We are both in the Spirit of God now, my dear. Why don't you look at me?" I replied, "I cannot look, Father, because your eyes are flashing like lightning. Your face has become brighter than the sun . . ." Father Seraphim said, "Don't be alarmed, your Godliness! Now you yourself have become as bright as I am. You are now in the fullness of the Spirit of God yourself; otherwise you would not be able to see me."[11]

In this section we have focused on the novelty that Christ brings to the original manifestation of God in Paradise. The God revealed by Christ is Father, Son, and Holy Spirit; he is "the one who Loves, the Beloved, and the Love itself."[12] The Son receives everything from the Father, and He returns everything to Him in the perfect unity of the Holy Spirit, who is the bond of union between them. This dynamic movement of love in God himself opens a gateway for the life story of the *imago Dei*, which enters by this door into God's own inner space.

Thus, although "the Beginning and the End are invisible," they become visible in the trajectory of human love over time, which we have summed up in three steps. First, Adam realizes that, even as a grown man, he is still a child who never ceases to come forth from the Father. Second, he understands that he must return to the Father by accepting the gift of Eve and giving himself to her. Third, the fecundity of Adam and Eve's union attests that the Love they share transcends them: "I have gotten a man with the help of the LORD" (Gen. 4:1). These three steps lead us to an astonishing conclusion: The family, which contains the whole genealogy of the person from childhood to marriage and parenthood, is called to be an image of the Trinity. The complete image of God is neither the soul, nor even the individual who is made up of body and soul, but a communion of persons participating in, and bearing witness to, God's own Trinitarian communion. As Adam puts it in *Reflections on Fatherhood*:

"If I knew how to implant myself in Him, I would find in myself the Love that fills Him. It is the love that reveals the Father in the Son and the Father, through the Son, gives birth to the Bridegroom" (*Ref Fath*, 368).

Adam and Eve's journey toward the fulfillment of their call to love leads them into the very heart of Trinitarian communion. This insight brings us to the end of the first part of our book. But it also leaves us with a question: How are we supposed to make this journey in our turn? Even if our bodies do somehow reveal the mystery of God, don't they still fall infinitely short of God's absolute transcendence? And even if that problem were solved, isn't the path to God obstructed by our sinful rejection of his love? Clearly, the answer to these difficulties has to come from above. Only a deeper consideration of the mystery of Christ, who is the unique Image that fully manifests the truth about man, can bring us closer to the solution. This contemplation of Christ is the task we will pursue in the second part of this book.

Part II

THE REDEMPTION OF THE HEART

CHAPTER 5

A WOUNDED HEART: THE FRAGILITY OF LOVE

THE FIRST PART OF THIS BOOK OPENED WITH JOHN PAUL II's image of a mountain stream flowing to join the sea. The rushing water prompted him to ask: "What do you say to me, mountain stream? Where do you encounter me?" (*RT*, 7). Our effort to understand the pope's answer to this question has brought home to us the difference between man's journey and the existence of inanimate things. As Saint Augustine puts it, "a body by its weight tends to move towards its proper place . . . Water poured on top of oil sinks below the oil . . . They are acted on by their respective densities, they seek their own place . . . My weight is my love. Wherever I am carried, my love is carrying me."[1] The human person differs from the other animals because his very existence is a response to a call to love, a call that evokes wonder in his heart and sets him on a quest for unknown horizons.

It goes without saying that man's journey isn't free of peril, and that the way of love is not as smooth as the flow of the stream rushing to meet its goal. In the words of Adam, the Everyman character from *The Jeweler's Shop*:

I could see
the whole span of human love
and its precipitous edges.
When someone slips over such an edge
he finds it very hard to get back,
and wanders alone below the road he should be on. (*JS*, 53)

We are all familiar with the perilous precipices human love must negotiate. Of course, everything seems easy at the beginning, when our feelings eagerly lead the way. In the warmth of its first glow, love seems to be

something indisputable,
a melody played on all
the strings of the heart. (*JS*, 51)

Later on, however, the difficulties set in and we learn just how fragile both we and those whom we love really are: "The strings become gradually muted," and we are "removed further and further away / from the pure taste of enthusiasm" (*JS*, 51). At this point, we have to wonder: Is it still possible to continue our journey of love? Or is our love like fireworks, which illumine the night sky for an instant but can't provide any lasting warmth and light?

What are we to make of love's grand promise of a rich future? If we want to learn to trust love's voice and discern its music, we need to be aware that other voices resound in our heart and threaten to fill us with disruptive noise. The melody of gift isn't the only sound that resonates in our lives. We know from experience that the cacophony of brokenness, even of evil, often threatens to drown out the call to true fulfillment. We need to be on our guard against this strain of disharmony; naïveté about the dangers we face on our journey is the last thing we can afford if we really wish to reach our destination.

In other words, the walls of love's dwelling turn out on closer inspection to be full of cracks. We have to ask ourselves whether we can have any real hope of lasting love in such a shaky edifice. Can't we all identify with Anna, who in *The Jeweler's Shop* describes the rift between her and her husband, Stefan? Aren't we all wounded like she is by an "inner crack in love . . . the rift, and the wound which hurts" (*JS*, 54)?

> I could not reconcile myself to this,
> nor could I prevent
> a rift opening between us
> (its edges stood still at first,
> but at any moment they could move apart
> wider and wider). (*JS*, 47)

Anna has identified a "rift" that threatens to pull asunder everything love has joined: man and the Creator, male and female, parent and child, even man and his very self. Our task now is to explore the concentric ripples that emanate from this rift to trouble the waters of love. Our guide in this exploration will be the biblical account of sin, since sin is the ultimate source of our dispersion and fragmentedness. As we already saw in Part I, the Bible sheds light on our most fundamental experiences as human beings, the wonder before the gift of creation and the call to love. Here, though, we'll be focusing on how the Bible illuminates the estrangement and disintegration that often seem to frustrate this call to love.

THE RIFT BETWEEN MAN AND GOD

The apostle John classifies under three headings the noise that prevents our hearts from hearing the music of love: the "concupiscence of the flesh," the "concupiscence of the eyes," and the "pride of life" (1 John 2:16). John adds that this "static" does not come from the Father, but from the world (1 John 2:17). The apostle's words seem obvious, but they immediately raise a question. For if the world comes entirely from God the Father, who saw that everything he had made was good, and if man's vocation is to receive the world as the Father's gift, how can John draw a contrast between what comes from the Father and what comes from the world? The answer to this question brings us back to the point in the book of Genesis where the covenant with the Father is broken in man's heart for the first time.

According to the Genesis account, the rift Anna talks about in *The Jeweler's Shop* originated with man's attempt to cut his ties with God, the Source of every gift. In Genesis 3 we see the beginning of this rift in man's temptation to mistrust the goodness of God: "Did God really tell you," the serpent whispers, "Did God say, 'You shall not eat of any tree in the garden'?" (Gen. 3:1). Notice how the serpent subtly accuses God of forbidding man access to "any of the trees" in Paradise. This accusation is, of course, a lie: God did *not* forbid man to eat from all the trees of the Garden; he *gave* Adam and Eve the whole of its verdant expanse, with the exception of the one tree whose fruit would be fatal to them. Nonetheless, the serpent has done his work of insinuating a plausible caricature of God as a tyrant who is out to prevent man from attaining true life. The question can no longer be avoided: Does God really love man?

"And the woman said to the serpent, 'We may eat of the fruit of the trees of the garden; but God said, "You shall not eat of the fruit of the tree which is in the midst of the garden, neither shall you touch it, lest you die" ' " (Gen. 3:2–3).

Eve's reply to the serpent seems to repudiate the false accusation, but her answer shows that she has already accepted the diabolical language of mistrust. Eve states that God forbade the first couple even to touch the tree in the middle of the garden, that is, the tree of life, but this claim is inaccurate. They were forbidden only to eat from the tree of the knowledge of good and evil, which the biblical account carefully distinguishes from the tree of life (see Gen. 2:9). The tree of the knowledge of good and evil is in fact different from the tree of life: It stands for a false independence based on the attempt to determine the meaning of existence without God, to be a self-sufficient spring with no need to draw the water of life from the original Source. The fruit of this tree, by separating man from God, does not bring abundance but only decay and death.

The serpent's temptation, however, consists precisely in blurring the distinction in Adam's and Eve's minds between the tree of the knowledge of good and evil and the tree of life.[2] The purpose of this maneuver, of course, is to make the first couple doubt God's goodness. After all, if the two trees really *were* identical, then the Creator's commandment to avoid the tree of the knowledge of good and evil would be a blatant tactic designed to hold man back from attaining the fullness of life. How could the Creator be good if he were envious of man's happiness? The truth, of course, is that the two trees are not at all identical, and that the Creator had planned all along to let man eat from the tree of life. God is not envious but generous, and he wishes man to live forever in the joy that comes from the acceptance of the divine gift.

The serpent's lie is that man can truly live only by deciding for himself what is good and what is evil. Consequently, John Paul II characterizes the original sin of Adam and Eve as a denial of the Father. Adam and Eve succumb to the temptation to think of God, not as the origin of the gift, but as an aloof dictator who protects his omnipotence by keeping everyone else at arm's length. They believe that God is hoarding the fullness of life, since they mistakenly think God is jealous of his own solitude; they, too, jealously seek isolation in their misguided effort to be like their false image of the Creator: "He is lonely, I thought. What will make me more like Him, that is to say, independent of everything? Ah, to stand apart from everything, so that I could be only within myself! . . . For I want to have everything through myself, not through You" (*RF*, 336–37).

In Poland, when a child is asked who he is, he answers by pointing out where he lives. The home gives the child his identity. It enables him to recognize who he is. Using the same logic in reverse, we could say that the Fall deprives Adam and Eve of their home and thus of their condition as children of God. Or better said, they themselves abandon Paradise, for they cease to experience the world as a home and lose their own identity in the process. Before man is cast out of Paradise, he has already cast God out of his heart: "By casting doubt in his heart on the deepest meaning of the gift, that is, on love as the specific motive of creation and of the original covenant, man turns his back on God-love, on the 'Father.' He in some sense casts him from his heart" (*TOB*, 237).

As John Paul II (citing 1 John 2:16) puts it, Adam and Eve follow a voice that no longer comes from the Father, but from the world. Before the Fall, the world spoke to man with the Father's voice; after the Fall, the cacophony and discord of the world seem to drown out the voice of God. Man's eyes, blinded by the doubt the serpent casts on the divine gift, no longer see the world in its true light; when these eyes look at other people and things, they no longer see an expression of God's love; they see everything through a lens of autonomous self-assertion that is opposed to, and shuts out, the face of Fatherhood.

We asked earlier how the apostle John's negative description of the world squares with the goodness of creation. The answer, we now see, is that the Fall changes man's relation to the world. Adam and Eve no longer perceive the world as a gift; they regard it merely as a collection of nameless and faceless objects. By the same token, they no longer receive the measure of their identity from the Father, but seek to measure themselves by the standard of these anonymous things that now populate the world for them. Man's adoption of a new and false standard for gauging his worth gives birth to what John calls "concupiscence," the voice whispering in man's heart that the world is not a gift to be received but a possession to be grasped. Driven by concupiscence, fallen man behaves as if there were no gift, *etsi donum non daretur*, to give the temptation its Latin name. The irony is that what man's snatching fingers close around is not life, but the disintegration of it: Just as accepting God's gift unified the whole of man's experience, the primal refusal of it introduces a rift between man and God that tears human life asunder on every level, as we will now see.

THE BODY:
FROM HOME TO PRISON

The first consequence of fallen man's refusal to accept the world as a gift affects the way in which he subsequently experiences his own body. To make this clear let's recall some key facts about the body that we learned in the first part of the book. We said that the body is our presence in the world and our encounter with reality. In consequence, living in the body means accepting our openness to, and dependence on, other people and things. This dependence should not be despised as a sheer limitation but welcomed as a chance for growth and transformation beyond the narrow confines of the self. The body, then, reveals to us that our existence is a gift and enables us to answer the Creator's generosity through a loving self-gift in return. John Paul II writes, "This is the body: a witness to creation as a fundamental gift, and therefore a witness to Love as the source from which this same giving springs" (*TOB*, 183).

The upshot of all this is that our appreciation of the meaning of the body stands and falls with our awareness of having received our life as a gift. Conversely, if you want to forget that your existence is a gift, then you need to silence the language of the body and drown out its testimony to Love. Adam and Eve experience this firsthand: In their effort to suppress the gift character of reality, they are obliged to ignore the language of the body. It is no wonder, then, that the Fall inclines them to forget that they *are* their bodies; they no longer regard their bodies as a home or a temple, but flee as from a prison or even as from a tomb. Fallen man constantly forgets that the body is "the region of freedom," as Benedict XVI defines it (*DCE*, 5); instead fallen man regards the body as a jail cell, as a limitation on his freedom and a curtailment of his possibilities. Our own culture typically deals with the body in this way, treating it as if it were some *thing* outside us, whose existence we accept only to the extent that it provides pleasure, but which we reject as soon as it becomes a source of pain or an obstacle to our desires.

When God asks Adam, "Where are you?" immediately after the Fall, Adam answers: "I was afraid . . . and I hid myself" (Gen. 3:10). Here is John Paul II glossing this passage of Scripture: "The words,

'I was afraid, because I am naked, and I hid myself,' attest to a radical change ... Man in some way loses the original certainty of the 'image of God' expressed in his body" (*TOB*, 241–42). Because it extinguishes the awareness of gift this alienation from our status as divine image also alienates us from our bodies. This alienation from our bodies in turn distorts our encounter with reality. Besides losing the certainty that God's image is expressed in his body, the pope tells us, man

> also loses in a certain way the sense of his right to participate in the perception of the world, which he enjoyed in the mystery of creation ... The words of Genesis 3:10, "I was afraid, because I am naked, and I hid myself," confirm the collapse of the original acceptance of the body as a sign of the person in the visible world. (*TOB*, 241–42)

Let's pause for a moment to ponder this important passage. The Fall, John Paul II tells us, has altered man's experience of his body for the worse. And this alteration puts a negative spin on man's presence in the physical world. The body, remember, is meant to be a home in which we gladly receive the world as a friend. Logically, then, our alienation from the body leaves us feeling like strangers in the world. Man no longer experiences his contact with the world as the reception of a gift, but as a risky exposure to a dangerous threat. The Fall, as John Paul tells us, fills us with a "cosmic shame" that makes us feel out of place, defenseless, and full of insecurity "in the face of the processes of nature that operate with an inevitable determinism" (*TOB*, 242). Man's original harmony with creation is broken, and it is replaced by mutual enmity; like the body, the world becomes a threat instead of a home. Accordingly, man also misunderstands the meaning of his dominion over the world. He no longer receives this dominion as a mission of love and care,[3] but abuses his charge as an opportunity for tyranny and exploitation. We suspect the world as if it were an enemy, and we attempt to subjugate it before it subjugates us.

A RIFT WITHIN MAN

So far we've seen how man's separation from God, through the Fall, leaves him radically homeless in and estranged from the world. As John Paul II puts it, God is the "place of the whole, dwelling on all encounters and of all men. Outside you [God] they are homeless."[4] Where, then, does man turn when he has left God behind? "Whither shall I go from thy Spirit? Or whither shall I flee from thy presence?" (Ps. 139:7).

Fallen man's answer to the Psalmist's question is itself an expression of the Fall: He seeks refuge from his broken relationship with God in the isolation of his own self; he attempts to secure his own identity apart from the Creator. Yet not even man's own inner self can shield him from God's presence. The Psalm we quoted at the end of the last paragraph thus continues: "Whither shall I go from thy spirit? . . . Thou knowest me right well; my frame was not hidden from thee" (Ps. 139:7, 14–15). Fallen man finds no refuge from the shame of brokenness in his inner self, because the problem introduced by the Fall affects precisely man's inner self. After all, since the body is not a mere possession or instrument outside me but *is* me, separation from the divine Source of my bodily existence is also separation from myself. The rift caused by my separation from God cuts through my whole being.

Another way of putting this is that the rift of sin wounds us to the heart. John Paul II defines the heart as the organ for perceiving the meaning of the body (see *TOB*, 231); the heart reveals to us the presence of the gift inscribed in our bodies. The heart, John Paul says, teaches us that the body is made to manifest love, even if it instructs us how to incarnate this love in our bodily actions. Consequently, whenever the gift character of the body is obscured, the heart is divided. Once divided in heart, I am no longer able to will anything with my whole being but am embroiled in a constant interior struggle with my very self. In the words of Saint Augustine, "I was in conflict with myself and was dissociated from myself."[5] And again: "How fearful a fate for the rash soul which nursed the hope that after it had departed from you, it would find something better! Turned this way and that, on its back, on its side, on its stomach, all positions are uncomfortable. You alone are repose."[6]

Man's inner brokenness, the wound he himself has inflicted on his own heart, generates what John Paul II calls "immanent shame," a shame generated within man's own self. The character Wojtyla calls "the Woman" in *Radiation of Fatherhood* describes this shame in an important passage of the play:

> Ah, Adam! . . . People born of him live in inner darkness, without expectations . . . They clothe themselves on the outside with an immense wealth of creatures and of their own work, but on the inside they are naked. Yet they are ashamed. So they run away, shouting, "I have hidden away because I am naked." (*RF*, 361)

"On the inside they are naked": These words capture the sense of interior or immanent shame that arises when we are alienated from our own bodies. We feel naked on the inside because we cannot control our reactions to the world, reactions that are out of synch with our own dignity. Our urges threaten to constrain our freedom, jeopardizing the very possibility of self-possession that enables us to be fully ourselves:

> The body is not subject to the spirit as in the state of original innocence, but carries within itself a constant hotbed of resistance against the spirit and threatens in some way man's unity as a person, that is, the unity of the moral nature that plunges its roots firmly into the very constitution of the person. The concupiscence of the body is a specific threat to the structure of self-possession and self-dominion, through which the human person forms itself. (*TOB*, 244)

Immanent shame sets us up for a further rift. Before the Fall, Eve's very presence embodied a call to love for Adam, just as he embodied a call to love for her. After the Fall, however, the two see each other in the harsh light of a world that they no longer experience as a gift. Unwilling to receive themselves from the hands of God, they accordingly lose the exercise of self-possession. But then, how can they give themselves to each other? The fact is, they no longer can, at least not fully, because the loss of their awareness of the primordial Giver contaminates their openness to each other. This brings us to what John Paul II calls the "relational dimension of shame," which we will unfold throughout the next section.

A Rift Between Man and Woman

The body is the meeting place between Adam and Eve: "This is flesh of my flesh," the first man says on seeing the first woman. The original unity that enabled the first couple to become one flesh likewise revealed them as the Creator's gift to each other. Predictably, when Adam and Eve forget the original Giver and lose the experience of the body as a home, this loss spills over into their unity with each other and impairs their ability to build up a common home in the communion of persons. Let us consider how this fatal logic of disunity works.

The Detachment of Spousal Love from Its Source

The first effect of the Fall is to separate the love between the spouses from the love of the original Giver. In the depth of their relationship, Adam and Eve are seized by an anxious fear of God (see *TOB*, 238). This fear generates in its turn the temptation to seal their love off from the Creator and to elevate it into an "absolute" apart from him. The result is an exclusive focus on each other, a self-contained couplehood isolated from the Source (and also from the rest of the world). Whereas they were originally "suitable helpmates" in a common search for God, Adam and Eve now attempt to erect a self-contained bubble in which they have eyes only for each other. As Adam puts it in *The Jeweler's Shop*, "You don't feel the spring but are consumed by the flame" (*JS*, 64). In another passage of the play, Adam frames the problem of self-contained couplehood in terms of the contrast between the surface of a stream and the deep currents beneath it:

The divergence between what lies on the surface and the mystery of love constitutes precisely the source of the drama. It is one of the greatest dramas of human existence. The surface of love has its current—swift, flickering, changeable. A kaleidoscope of waves and situations full of attraction. This current is sometimes so stunning that it carries people away—women and men. They get carried away by the thought that they have absorbed the whole secret of love, but in fact they have not yet even touched it. They are happy for a while, thinking they have reached the limits of existence and wrested all its secrets from it. (*JS*, 58)

The Mutual Estrangement of Man and Woman

Once man ceases to draw from the Source of the gift, he can no longer give himself to another person in the truth of love. His body unlearns the language of gift, and he begins to experience his own flesh more as a barrier that separates than as a bridge that connects. As a consequence, man's emotions no longer reliably attune him to the beloved's interior world but tend to distort and cloud his perception of it. Needless to say, without trustworthy mutual knowledge, man and woman inevitably fall short of the truth of their one-flesh union and miss out on real love. While man continues to perceive the promise built into his desire to love, he no longer knows how to fulfill this desire through genuine self-giving to another person.

Man and woman may try to seal off their mutual relationship from God, but this attempt undermines their relationship with each other. Separated from the Source of love, the partners render themselves unable to share in a common world. Wojtyla illustrates this point in a scene from *The Jeweler's Shop* where Anna complains of her husband, Stefan's, indifference to the wound of her loneliness: "He could not heal the wound that had opened in my soul. It did not hurt him, he did not feel it . . . Will it heal of itself? But if it heals of itself, it will still somehow separate us" (*JS*, 48). Adam echoes the same lament in *Radiation of Fatherhood*: "Too many of the bonds between us are external; there are too few inner bonds . . . you live too little in me, though you are so close" (*RF*, 356).

The Breakdown of Mutual Self-Giving

When man and woman are separated from the Source of love and are unable to share in a common world, the relationship between them further deteriorates. Again, the root of the problem lies in man's diminished awareness of God's gift and his impaired capacity to receive himself from the hands of the Creator. Because he is no longer fully able to receive himself from God, man cannot possess himself fully either. Moreover, damaged acceptance of God's gift entails the impairment of man's capacity to enter into the world of the beloved. Adam comes to regard Eve as alien to his being, and she comes to regard him as alien to hers.

Consequently, the two gradually cease to treat each other as individual people, and increasingly they reduce each other to objects in a world already populated by faceless things with no meaning. Adam and Eve no longer fully perceive each other as human persons who differ from the rest of creation. They see each other more and more as merely a part of the natural world that, as we saw just now, has lost its character of gift.

The very fact that fallen men and women tend to treat each other as objects or as a means of satisfaction awakens a new sense of shame that did not trouble them before the Fall. That is, the very existence of practically uncontrollable urges to mutual domination and exploitation arouses a corresponding sense of shame. Although this shame is necessary as a defense mechanism against fallen man's disordered propensities, which degrade the call to true love, it is nonetheless a sign of his incapacity to possess himself fully and to give himself in love. The result is an inner disharmony that generates and feeds shame, not only within ourselves, but in our relationships with one another. With that we come to the core of the relational dimension of shame. Let's explore this idea more fully.

The Logic of Domination Versus the Logic of Gift

The shame generated by disordered inclinations inside the person goes hand in hand with a second kind of shame. This other side of shame is like a veil that we don as a protection against the greedy stare of those who would reduce us to an object for their own enjoyment. This other face of shame does not concern *our* feelings; it defends us against the feelings of *others* who regard us with lust. It is a defense against the logic of domination that, according to the book of Genesis, sin introduces into the world: "your desire," God says to the woman after the Fall, "shall be for your husband, and he shall rule over you" (Gen. 3:16). Here is John Paul II commenting on this scriptural passage in his apostolic letter *Mulieris Dignitatem*:

> Biblical "knowledge" is achieved in accordance with the truth of the person only when the mutual self-giving is not distorted either by the desire of the man to become the "master" of his wife ("he shall rule over you") or by the woman remaining

closed within her own instincts ("your desire shall be for your husband": Gen. 3:16). (*MD*, 18)

The key point John Paul II makes in this passage is that sin brings disorder into both the male and the female body, even though men and women experience this disruption differently, as we would expect given their different ways of being embodied. The man, for instance, typically seeks to rule over the woman and to measure her worth by the yardstick of his own sexual pleasure. This temptation lurks in the very physiognomy of his sexuality. To illustrate this point, take, for example, the fact that the link between sexuality and the procreation of a new life—and the mystery of the person associated with it—is external to the experience of male sexuality. Since men don't carry their children in their own bodies, the link between sex and the person tends to remain more "external" to their experience. If the man yields to this characteristic temptation, he spoils spousal love with an alien logic of master and slave, which turns the body into "a terrain of appropriation of the other person" (*TOB*, 261).

Men, then, are in danger of absolutizing sensuality in isolation from feeling and so of seeking loveless sex devoid of any tender regard for the value of the person. By contrast, women are much less likely to separate sex from the mystery of the person. They have more built-in protection against this temptation than man, because the link between sexuality and the origin of life is knit into the female body. Nevertheless, as John Paul II points out in the passage we cited just now from *Mulieris Dignitatem*, women also have to wrestle with a typical temptation of their own. If men are tempted to seek sensual gratification at the expense of feeling, women are in danger of getting trapped in their emotions. To be sure, emotions

often help women transcend an exclusive focus on mere sexual pleasure, but feelings can sometimes imprison them in a selfish habit of
measuring everything according to their own affections. Anna sums
up this characteristic female temptation in *The Jeweler's Shop*: "Isn't
the truth [simply] what one feels more strongly?" (*JS*, 56). To yield
to this temptation is to set aside the task of building a solid home for
love and to abandon oneself instead to the ebb and flow of sentiment
that by its nature can offer no firm ground for love to rest on (see *RF*,
357–58).

So far, we have focused on the different ways in which the replace-
ment of the logic of gift with the logic of domination affects man
and woman, respectively. It is important to stress, however, that the
tendency to domination does not merely wound each partner sepa-
rately; it also frustrates their unity. The logic of domination thrusts
both man and woman into a solitary egoism out of whose narrow
windows each looks at the other as a mere object. Note that the partners don't just selfishly exploit each other; they also let themselves be
treated as objects in their turn. The "pleasure" that gives this mutual
manipulation its superficial charm just barely covers over the enor-
mous ocean of bitter sadness lying underneath: "If a man relates to
a woman in such a way that he considers her only as an object to ap-
propriate and not as a gift, he condemns himself at the same time to
become, on his part too, only an object of appropriation for her and
not a gift" (*TOB*, 260).

The Abuse of Love as an Alibi:
Does Love Justify Everything?

The temptation to reduce another person to a mere object for one's
own satisfaction is common to man and woman, although each sex

experiences this temptation in its own characteristic way. This common temptation likewise bears a common fruit. For whether we identify love with sexual impulse like the man or with dazzling emotions like the woman, in either scenario we tend to treat this reduced version of love as an absolute that forces itself upon us and deprives us of any free initiative. Of course, this self-induced curtailment of our freedom presents us with a convenient excuse to justify everything we do in the name of the supposedly irresistible force of "love." The adulterer, for example, will defend the abandonment of spouse and children by invoking the allegedly overwhelming power of what he is pleased to call "love." Ironically, even self-proclaimed champions of absolute freedom will blithely confess man's absolute lack of freedom to resist the imperious demands of impulse or feeling.

In the *Divine Comedy* Dante strikingly illustrates this misuse of love as an alibi. As he journeys through the first circle of Hell, the poet encounters Paolo and Francesca, an adulterous couple who are locked forever in the embrace that united them in life. The dead lovers try to justify their sin by appealing to a supposed inability to resist their powerful mutual attraction. In Francesca's words,

"Love, which allows no loved one not to love,
Seized me with such a strong delight in him
that, as you see, it will not leave me yet."[7]

Paolo and Francesca are punished in Hell by being yoked together like dead leaves weightlessly tossed "here and there and up and down" by the ever-changing wind of desire.[8] The story of Paolo and Francesca illustrates what happens when we are wholly dominated by the push and pull of our attractions. When our so-called "love" is in permanent secession from the government of our free will, there can be no question of stable love or the promise of fidelity in our lives. Once the "strings become gradually muted" (*JS*, 51), lovers shrink from the rigors of faithfulness and submit instead to the caprice of a permanent itch for novelty. Needless to say, this restlessness prevents love from taking any deep root in our hearts, as Anna experiences in *The Jeweler's Shop*. Tired of her husband, Stefan, Anna is driven about aimlessly by her "longing for something different, different, different" (see *JS*, 56–57). Anna is like a sick woman racked by a fever who tosses and turns in restless agitation; her love is constantly in motion, but it bears no fruit.

A RIFT BETWEEN
PARENTS AND CHILDREN

The rift within man's heart, which also divides man and woman, cannot help but affect the children born from their love. In *The Jeweler's Shop*, Anna, wounded by the rift that has estranged her from her husband, contemplates her children in the painful certainty that, sooner or later, the rift will be passed on to them as well: "I was a mother. Every night our children went to sleep in the next room: Mark, who was the eldest, Monica and John. There was silence in the nursery: that rift in our love, which I felt so painfully, had not yet passed into the souls of the children" (*JS*, 49). Sadly, Anna is right: Later on in the play, Anna's daughter, Monica, laments her parents' lack of love and mourns the wound of fear that their estrangement has left in her soul:

My parents live like two strangers,
the union one dreams of does not exist,

where one person wants to accept, and to give, life for two . . .
Is human love at all
capable of enduring through man's whole existence?
Well, . . . [I am] pervaded by a feeling of the future,
and that is fear. (*JS*, 75)

These speeches from *The Jeweler's Shop* express Karol Wojtyla's conviction that children come from the love of their parents, and that any rift in parental love therefore leaves a mark on the children's souls, giving a negative slant to their whole attitude toward life. Needless to say, God's original plan for man was very different. The Creator's intention, as we know, was to show himself visibly in the love between parents, so that every child could glimpse the divine Fatherhood in his own human father and mother. Unfortunately, Adam and Eve refused to accept this awesome responsibility to manifest God's love in their love. Although parents continue to transmit the image of God to their children even after the Fall, the image is infected by a germ of loneliness that is perpetuated from generation to generation:

Adam, do you remember? In the beginning He asked,
"Where are you?"
And you answered: "I hid myself from You
because I was naked" . . .
All those who fill the main wall of the Sistine painting
bear in themselves the legacy of that reply of yours!
Such is the End of the path you trod. (*RT*, 23)

Human parenthood, then, has suffered a wound that compromises its ability to convey the fullness of God's Fatherhood and to transmit the awareness of life as a gift. The rift in man's heart has done its work: Adam "became lonely in order to graft that loneliness onto others" (*RF*, 336). The impairment of the radiation of Fatherhood entails an absence of the original grace that the Creator had originally intended for every child who comes into the world. As John Paul II puts it, "instead of being illumined by the heritage of original grace . . . procreation was darkened by the heritage of original sin" (*TOB*, 507). The question we have to ask ourselves before concluding this chapter is this: Where can we turn for light to illumine the rather dark landscape we've painted so far?

A CALL TO THE HUMAN HEART

The present chapter has focused mainly on the negative, exposing the wound in the human heart left by sin and the manifold rift this wound creates in its turn. If we're honest with ourselves, we realize that the wound of sin is not simply an occasional lapse or a regrettable tendency to surrender one's will to the force of passion. At the core of the divisions that wound our heart lurks man's craving to occupy the center of the universe without acknowledging the primordial gift he receives from the true Center. Man suffers from a lack of humility before the truth of love, the refusal to accept that our lives are a gift that we first receive from the Source:[9] "they do not try to connect that love with the Love that has such a dimension [the dimension of the Absolute]. They do not even feel the need, blinded as they are not so much by the force of their emotion as by lack of humility. They lack humility towards what love must be in its true essence" (*JS*, 88).

Our refusal of God's gift results, in turn, in the disorder the apostle John (along with Saint Paul) calls "concupiscence." As we've seen, this concupiscence is an effect of the first sin, and it has been passed down from generation to generation ever since the Fall first dimmed the radiation of God's Fatherhood in human love. We've all experienced this drowsiness that would close our eyes to the gift of our own lives, of other people, and of the world around us. Ever since the Fall, our eyes, swollen with pride, no longer see reality clearly. But is concupiscence the whole picture? Are we powerless to love?

John Paul II, echoing the entire Christian tradition, answers this question with a resounding no! The negative experience of sin, the pope teaches, does not reach as deeply into the fabric of our being as do the positive experiences we examined in the first part of this book. "Original solitude," "original unity," and "original nakedness," in John Paul's vision, are even more original than "original sin" itself. This confidence in the goodness of creation is not naive; it has the weight of Christian revelation behind it: The experience of love and grace is the only experience that is totally original, whereas evil came on the scene only afterward, mocking goodness, but never destroying it completely. John Paul's personal experience of the horrors of the twentieth century never shook his deep-rooted knowledge that the power of goodness is even greater than the power of evil (which, let us not forget, he had experienced firsthand with an intensity that most of us cannot even imagine):

> Why was it said about that one day alone:
> "God saw all that he had made and found it very good"?
> Is this not denied by history?
> Even our own twentieth century!

And not only the twentieth!
Yet no century can obscure this truth
of the image and likeness. (*RT*, 18)

Man is made in God's image and likeness, and this truth can never be totally obscured. Evil is a parasite that couldn't even exist if there weren't some prior goodness to rebel against. By the same token, we couldn't even know that we've failed unless we still had an inkling of the path to our goal. Even the wanderings of Anna—fallen away from love, on the brink of infidelity—are still full of yearning for someone who is to come: the Bridegroom. And, as Adam recounts in *The Jeweler's Shop*, Anna finally does meet this Bridegroom. Her encounter with him marks a new beginning in her love: "That evening I saw Anna again. The memory of her encounter with the Bridegroom was still vivid to her . . . The turning point occurred that night many years ago. At that time everything threatened destruction. A new love could begin only through a meeting with the Bridegroom" (*JS*, 87).

Yes, the Bridegroom has come. Not to condemn the human heart, but to renew God's original call and to inaugurate an answer to this vocation to love. Indeed, the Bridegroom himself has already answered the call for our sakes, giving us the hope of being able to answer it in our own name as well. It is to this hope brought by the Bridegroom that we turn in the next chapter.

Chapter 6

CHRIST: THE REDEEMER OF THE HEART AND THE FULLNESS OF LOVE

THE LAST CHAPTER'S SURVEY OF THE RIFT IN MAN'S HEART ended on a note of hope: The Bridegroom comes to heal us of our incapacity to love. Wojtyla makes extensive use of the image of the Bridegroom in his play *The Jeweler's Shop*. At one point in the play, for instance, Adam rouses Anna from forgetful slumber and prepares her to meet the Bridegroom: "I've wakened you," Adam tells her, "because the Bridegroom is to walk down this street. The wise virgins want to come forward and meet him with their lights . . . The Bridegroom is coming. This is his precise hour" (*JS*, 63–65). Recalling this scene later on in the play, Adam comments: "[For Anna] everything threatened destruction. A new love could begin only through a meeting with the Bridegroom" (*JS*, 87). Who, then, is this Bridegroom that comes to waken us from our sleep? Is he simply a character in Wojtyla's play, or does this character stand for a real Person who enables us to fulfill love's call beyond all our expectations?

We've come to a point in our reflections where this question takes on a particular urgency, since we can no longer ignore the obstacles we face in our efforts to respond to the call to love. The first obstacle,

as we saw in the last chapter, is the wound inflicted on the human
heart by sin, which potentially poisons every act of love. But sin isn't
the only problem. The very fact that love's ultimate destiny is union
with God himself, the Source and Origin of love, seems to pose a difficulty. For even granting that we are made in God's image and likeness, isn't the human heart still much too small a vessel to receive the
immense gift of God himself? Don't the limitations of our fragile,
mortal bodies render us incapable of imaging the fullness of divine
love?[1] Even if the wounded heart is healed, how can its expectations
be fulfilled? Can the image of God really be brought to perfection in
our fragile, finite bodies? Wojtyla beautifully formulates this question in *The Jeweler's Shop*:

> How can it be done, Teresa,
> for you to stay in Andrew forever?
> How can it be done, Andrew,
> for you to stay in Teresa forever
> since man will not endure in man
> and man will not suffice? (*JS*, 41)

As we might expect, man's search for an answer to these questions
leads him either out of himself or nowhere. Adam's journey to his
true identity began in wonder, and he can find the key to the mystery
of his existence only in the wonder of a new revelation. The call to
love is always a surprise, and a surprise is just what we need to get us
out of the dead end in which we find ourselves. The chance to start
again—if it's offered—must be a revelation and a grace that confirms
the universal human experience that love is an absolutely free and
surprising gift. In a word: Only the Bridegroom's coming can answer

our anxious questioning about the possibility of love. But who is this Bridegroom?

"Many have spoken about charity," says Maximus Confessor. But the disciples of Christ are privileged, "because only these have Charity itself as the teacher of charity."[2] The Bridegroom is Christ, whose life, death, and Resurrection fully manifest love. As Pope Benedict says, "It is from there that our definition of love must begin. In this contemplation the Christian discovers the path along which his life and love must move" (*DCE*, 11). Let's consider now how Christ offers us a new chance to resume our journey toward the fulfillment of the call to love.

RECOVERING FATHERHOOD

We've already seen that one of the two chief obstacles on the path of love is a refusal of what we've called the "original gift." It's important in order to understand everything that follows to bear in mind that this refusal is mainly a rejection of God's *Fatherhood*. Wojtyla's Everyman, Adam, highlights this no to divine paternity in *Radiation of Fatherhood*: "Can I ask, after all this, that You forgive me for executing my plan with such obstinacy? For continually evading Your Fatherhood and gravitating toward my loneliness, so that You must reveal Yourself as if in an external vacuum?" (*RF*, 338).

We recall from earlier chapters that God's original plan was to reveal his Fatherhood in the love of the first parents. In accord with this plan, Adam and Eve were to bear witness to the original Giver, and their mutual love was meant to embody the divine gift of life for their children. But because Adam and Eve excluded God from the core of their relationship, the Creator can no longer shine with total clarity through the prism of human parenthood. God's face still radiates, of course, but the lens it shines through distorts it. We now see a caricature of God, a Legislator who imposes an alien law on man's heart from outside the dynamic of love. God's Fatherhood is still visible at the heart of man's existence and vocation, but man has lost the eyes to see it. He no longer clearly perceives the Creator as the original Giver.

The image of God in man is not totally lost, however. "No century can obscure this truth of the image and likeness" (*RT,* 18). God works to imprint his image on the human heart once more and to reveal his Fatherhood in the midst of human history. He persistently searches for man, as the Bible records for us. This divine quest begins with the calling of Abraham:

> All that we know is that he heard a Voice,
> which told him: Go!
> Abram chose to follow the Voice
> The Voice said: You will be the father of many nations
> Your offspring will be numerous as the sand on the seashore.
>   (*RT,* 29)

God's call—"Go!"—signals a new beginning for Abraham. And not only for Abraham: When the Patriarch hearkens trustingly to the divine Voice, it's the whole human race that in him responds anew to the call to love. Abraham is man returning to filial obedience to the original Giver. Abraham also himself reveals to man a first inkling of God's own Fatherhood. In response to Abraham's filial obedience, God promises Abraham a new paternity: " 'Look toward heaven, and number the stars, if you are able to number them.

Just so,' he added, 'shall your descendants be' " (Gen. 15:5). "I will bless [Sarah, your wife], and moreover I will give you a son by her" (Gen. 17:16).

John Paul II imagines God's dialogue with Abraham in his *Roman Triptych*: "A son—which means: fatherhood and motherhood. / You will become a father, Abram, the father of many peoples" (*RT*, 32).

The pope continues with a dramatic re-creation of Abraham's reaction to the divine promise:

> How can this promise be fulfilled, thought Abram,
> since nature has denied me the gift of fatherhood?
> My wife, whom I have loved from the days of my youth,
> gave me no son. It pains us both.
> But the Voice kept saying: You will become a father,
> you will become the father of many nations.
> Your offspring will be numerous as the
> sand on the seashore. (*RT*, 30)

Although his wife, Sarah, was sterile, Abraham believed God's promise to raise up seed for him from Sarah's barren womb. Abraham's fatherhood, then, is rooted in his faith and in his trust in God's promise. By the same token, Abraham's fatherhood is an acknowledgment of the Source and an acceptance of the original Giver. Thanks to Abraham, whom Karol Wojtyla calls "the visible beginning of a new Adam" (*Collected Poems*, 114), God can radiate again in human fatherhood. Let us consider now how Christ brings to fulfillment the covenant of paternity that God first offered to man in Abraham.

CHRIST THE SON

Christians see the Old Testament as one long preparation for what Saint Paul calls "the fullness of time," when "God sent forth his Son" (Gal. 4:4) and so fulfilled in a surprising way the promises made to Abraham. It's fitting that the Son should be the one to usher in the "fullness of time" that restores the radiation of Fatherhood. This is because, as the story of Abraham shows, man cannot become a father unless he first becomes a son; human fatherhood is based on confidence in God the Father, who is the Source of all fatherhood. It's only when man accepts his identity as a child of God filled with the Father's love that he can radiate this love to his own children. As Karol Wojtyla puts it: "After a long time I came to understand that you do not want me to be a father unless I become a child. That is why Your Son came into the world. He is entirely Yours" (*RF*, 339).

This passage from *Radiation of Fatherhood* identifies the special privilege that distinguishes Jesus from all other human beings. Jesus belongs entirely to the Father: "He is entirely Yours." His existence consists in the pure act of coming from the Father and of referring totally to him: "My food is to do the will of him who sent me, and to accomplish his work" (John 4:34). These words from the Gospel of John sum up the core of Christian belief about Jesus's identity: Jesus, Christians proclaim, is the Son of God, who is eternally begotten of the Father and one in being ("consubstantial" is the technical term) with him. Put more simply, the Father eternally shares the complete divine nature with the Son, and the Son is therefore the same one God that the Father is. Jesus and the Father are not the same person, but they are the same one God.

In the fullness of time, the Son—while remaining God—also becomes man. In fact, he becomes the Prototype of true humanity. The Son comes to perform the mission proper to a son, which is to reveal the Father and his love (see *GS*, 22).

The Son's coming heals our blindness to God's paternity that Karol Wojtyla describes in *Radiation of Fatherhood*. At one point in the play, Adam expresses his belief that God "is lonely" and wonders "[w]hat will make me more like Him, that is to say, independent of everything? Ah, to stand apart from everything, so that I could be only within myself! I should then be closest to You" (*RF*, 336). By contrast, Christ, the new man and the eternal Son, says "[the Father] has not left me alone, for I always do what is pleasing to him" (John 8:29). God does not live in lonely solitude, as Wojtyla's Adam imagines: He has an eternal Son, who is one with him in total communion. It is this Son who opens the space of filiation for man. The Creator does not have to make room in himself for his creatures; the Son, who has always existed in the Father's heart, *is* that room in person (see *RT*, 13–17).

John Paul II observes that "through the fact that the Word of God became flesh, the body entered theology—that is, the science that has divinity for its object—I would say, through the main door."[3] But how can the Son, who is equal to the Father, take up a human body that is molded from the dust of the ground?

At this point we need to recall what we said in an earlier chapter about the language of the body. We argued that the body bespeaks dependence and vulnerability, but that this condition isn't a mere limitation, since it opens us to the world and our fellow human beings and so broadens the horizon of our lives. The vulnerability the body speaks of is a receptivity that enables us to experience every person and object of our world and every moment of our life as God's gift. Even more: The human body opens us to the Absolute and sets us on a journey (which takes a whole lifetime) toward personal communion with God.

Because the body's vulnerability is openness to God, it is not foreign to the Son. Rather the body, being made for communion with the original Giver, is a perfect vehicle for expressing Jesus's identity as the Father's only begotten Son. The Son himself is total openness and receptivity to the Father, and the Son's filial attitude eliminates any possible conflict between his divine identity and his flesh. On the one hand, the incarnate Son's flesh displays his essential communion with the Father. On the other hand, the Incarnation doesn't destroy human bodily nature but perfects it and manifests its full truth. *Indeed, Christ's existence perfects the language of the body, fully revealing its true nature as relationship with the Father, dependence on him, and acceptance of his gift.*

Therefore, Christ's fulfillment of the body's language is the highest expression of original solitude. Original solitude, remember, is based on the fact that, from the very first moment of its existence, the body is a sign revealing the Giver as the origin and destiny of life. The Incarnation takes this revelation and raises it to a whole new level; the Son becomes man in order to show us in his own body the paternal face of the original Giver: "He who has seen me has seen the Father" (John 14:9). Christ's Sonship restores the original meaning of the body as a manifestation of God, even as he integrates this manifestation into his eternal filial relation to the Father. Christ fully reveals the true face of original solitude, which is the face of Sonship (see *TOB*, 190–91).[4]

The central role of the body in the Incarnation is mirrored in the special dignity of Mary, whom the Church venerates as the Mother of God. Mary's act of conceiving and bearing the Son without loss of her virginity restores the meaning of motherhood as total openness toward God's gift of life. Wojtyla stresses that this motherhood reveals the divine paternity: "Motherhood," he writes, "is an expression of fatherhood. It must always go back to the father to take from him all that it expresses. In this consists the radiation of fatherhood" (*RF*, 341). In Mary, God's fatherhood radiates anew from the heart of human parenthood, and Mary is rightfully called "the new Eve." Mary is the new "mother of all living" (Gen. 3:20) who is uniquely entitled to say: "I have gotten a man with the help of the LORD" (Gen. 4:1).

Christ reopens to us the way of childhood and enables us to become sons and daughters of his Father: "One returns to the father through the child," says Mother in *Radiation of Fatherhood* (*RF*, 341). In its turn, the restoration of childhood heals the broken relationships of spouses who have forgotten the original Giver. In *The Jeweler's Shop*, the Bridegroom reconciles Anna and Stefan by reawakening their memory of the gift of filiation. As Stefan says: "What a pity that for so many years we have not felt ourselves to be a couple of children. / Anna, Anna, how much we have lost because of that" (*JS*, 91).

The attentive reader will notice that we've suddenly shifted from calling Christ "the Son" to calling him "the Bridegroom." Does Jesus just happen to have these two names, or is there some more essential connection between them?

CHRIST THE BRIDEGROOM

We've said that the body speaks of the Father's gift and of our dependence on him. But the body also enables us to enter into communion with others. It is a gateway to the experience of other people through which we join them in transforming the world into a common home. Similarly, the Son's entrance into our bodily condition makes it possible for us to encounter him in our humanity and to share in his human experience. The Son of God was born of a woman and became our brother, flesh of our flesh. As the Letter to the Hebrews puts it: "Since the children of the family share in blood and flesh, he likewise shared in them" (Heb. 2:14), "becoming like his brothers in every way" (Heb. 2:17). By assuming flesh, Christ, the Son of God, became our brother.

In order to grasp the full import of Christ's identification with us—and to explain how the Son is also a Bridegroom—we need to recall an important aspect about the relationship between Adam and Eve. It doesn't fully dawn on them that God is the Father, the Source of all gifts, until they stand face-to-face with each other as the Creator's gifts to each other. In loving each other, then, Adam and Eve love God, the original Giver, and enter into a covenant with him. Another way of saying the same thing is that original unity enriches original solitude; our relationship with one another gives us a firmer hold on our own identity as God's children. Original solitude and original unity are like two sides of the same coin we call the human person, as we saw in chapter 3's discussion about the gift.

Christ comes to recover man's original experiences and to reawaken us to the call to love. In order to do that, he enters into both our solitude and our unity, both our relationship to God and our communion with one another. Christ shows his love for the Father precisely by "[loving] his own . . . in the world [and loving] them to the end" (see John 13:1). But how, exactly, does Christ's life unite original solitude (his reference to the Father) and original unity (his communion with his disciples)? Karol Wojtyla gives us an important clue in a poem in which he pictures Christ's body as the "space" in which Christ both *gives himself to us* and *accepts us* as a gift from the Father (see *Collected Poems*, 116). We'll briefly consider Jesus's acceptance of, and self-gift to, us in what follows.

"Those You Gave Me" (John 17:6) — We Are Accepted by Christ

At the Last Supper, Christ says to the Father: "I have manifested thy name to the men whom thou gavest me out of the world; thine they were, and thou gavest them to me, and they have kept thy word" (John 17:6). These words reveal Jesus's keen sense that the disciples are a gift he receives from the hand of the Father. Christ lives out his relationship to the Father precisely by accepting the disciples into his care.

Christ's acceptance of his disciples casts the relationship between Adam and Eve into a new context. Before the Fall, God called Adam to welcome Eve into his care, and vice versa. By accepting each other from God, moreover, Adam and Eve affirmed each other's dignity. They were in effect saying to each other something similar to what Christ would say to his disciples: "You are precious to God, who has entrusted you to my care. You are a human being, the only creature on earth whom God loves for his own sake" (see *GS*, 24).

It goes without saying that Christ doesn't simply repeat the story of Adam and Eve gesture for gesture. He fulfills their experience of original unity, but he also crowns it in an unexpected way. Because he is the eternal Son of the Father, his "expertise" in affirming all the Father's gifts is the core of his very divine identity: "The Father loves the Son and *has given all things into his hand*" (John 3:35). Christ's identity as the eternal Son made man empowers him to affirm the dignity of the human person with a commitment whose fidelity infinitely exceeds the mutual yes of Adam and Eve before the Fall. Christ's love does not falter even in the face of man's sin, contempt, and hatred, "For the Son of Man came to seek and to save the lost" (Luke 19:10).

"God . . . Gave His Only Son" (John 3:16) — Christ Is Given to Us

Not only are we the Father's gift to Christ; Christ is also the Father's gift to us. The Gospel of John assures us of this: "God so loved the world that he gave his only Son" (John 3:16). Christ is the only Son, the Beloved of the Father, whom the Father sent into the world to save us. By contemplating Christ, we come to understand the love God has for us.

Being God's gift to the world, Christ brings to fulfillment the experience Adam and Eve enjoyed in Paradise. For just as our first parents were called to be gifts to each other, Christ is the Father's supreme gift to us. Once again, Christ's way of fulfilling the encounter between Adam and Eve is unexpected and surprising, for Christ is the Father's only Son. The Son sums up all the Father can give; once he has sent the Son to us, the Father has no further gift to bestow, for the gift of the Son is already the fullest possible manifestation of his paternal love. In *Roman Triptych*, John Paul II uses the sacrifice of Abraham to illustrate the fullness of the Father's gift:

> For God revealed to Abraham
> what it means for a father to sacrifice his own son—a sacrificial
>   death.
> Abraham—God so loved the world

that he gave his only Son, that all who believe in Him
should have eternal life. (*RT,* 35)

Christ's self-gift to us, and his acceptance of us in turn, reconnects original solitude (we are God's children) and original unity
(we are called to become spouses). This restoration of the fullness
of gift explains, in turn, how Christ's Sonship shades over naturally
into his Bridegroom's role. On the one hand, just as Adam accepted
and affirmed Eve as a gift from God, Christ totally accepts and affirms humanity as the Father's gift. Christ's loving affirmation of
"the men [the Father] gavest" him (see John 17:6) renews our sense
of the value and dignity of our lives. As Saint Leo the Great says:
"Acknowledge, oh Christian, your dignity."[5] On the other hand, just
as we have been accepted by Christ, we are invited to accept him in
turn as the Father's total gift of paternal love for humanity. Just as
the New Adam's acceptance of us transforms us collectively into a
New Eve, a Bride "without spot or wrinkle or any such thing" (Eph.
5:27), our acceptance of him introduces us into the ascending spiral
of spousal love that leads us up toward the Father in the Son. In a
word: The Son is also a Bridegroom because he fulfills—in a surprising way—the double movement of spousal love that unfolds through
the mutual giving and receiving between man and wife.

"THIS IS MY BODY WHICH IS GIVEN FOR YOU" (SEE LUKE 22:19)

So far we have looked at the dynamism of the gift, but we must now
say a word about how sin obscures its meaning. As we saw in chap-

ter 5, man no longer lives simply according to the logic of the gift; man is subject to a fallen logic of domination, which threatens to isolate him in loneliness and interrupt his journey toward the fullness of love. Instead of treating the body as a gift, fallen man tends to abuse it as a "terrain of appropriation" (*TOB*, 261) whose only law is mutual manipulation. This analysis of our fallen situation has a sobering corollary: Because love runs counter to the logic of domination, the genuine lover is bound to suffer. Anyone who wants to love must face the possibility of indifference and rejection; he must be willing to suffer on account of the fractured unity of human existence: "Loneliness opposes love. On the borderline of loneliness, love must become suffering: Your Son has suffered" (*RF*, 339).

The experience of suffering is a consequence of sin, because sin ruptured the original harmony that existed before the Fall of man. Nevertheless, suffering also has a special capacity to reveal love. As Karol Wojtyla wrote in one of his early plays, "from suffering rises a New Covenant" (*Job*, 70). This mysterious connection between suffering and love is the key to the recovery of man's original vocation.

Sooner or later, suffering always compels us to ask whether life has any meaning. But to whom is this question addressed? According to John Paul II, the ultimate addressee of our anguished query about suffering is God.[6] Suffering is a testament to man's original solitude before the Creator. The suffering body painfully relearns the language of original solitude, as Dostoyevsky shows us in a scene from *The Brothers Karamazov*:

The elder [father Zossima] suddenly rose from his place . . . stepped towards Dmitri Fyodorovich and, having come close to him, knelt before him. Alyosha thought for a moment that he had fallen from weakness, but it was something else. Kneeling in front of Dmitri Fyodorovich, the elder bowed down at his feet with a full, distinct, conscious bow, and even touched the floor with his forehead.[7]

Later on, Zossima explains this gesture to Dmitri's brother Alyosha: "I bowed yesterday to his great future suffering."[8] Suffering is a foil that throws into relief the sacred dimension of the human person; it reveals to us the mystery in man and moves us to kneel before it.

The suffering body, then, speaks the language of original solitude. But it also speaks the language of original unity and so establishes communion. The sight of a suffering person moves us to compassion, inviting us to share in his suffering. John Paul II speaks in this regard of a "world of suffering" (see *Salvifici Doloris*, 5–8). In fact, suffering is a way of sharing the world with one another, and this communion is in turn the key to the meaning of suffering: "[S]uffering is present in the world in order to release love, in order to give birth to works of love towards neighbor, in order to transform the whole of human civilization into a 'civilization of love' " (*Salvifici Doloris*, 30).

The spectacle of suffering is a call to love the sufferer and to enter into union with him. When we accept this call, love shines forth anew in the world. This irradiation of love is itself the answer to the question of human suffering. Love transforms suffering; what was formerly just a consequence of sin now becomes the first step toward overcoming it.[9]

Suffering is a language of the body that speaks of original solitude and original unity in one breath. This language finds its most eloquent expression in the life of Christ, the true Good Samaritan who is moved to compassion by the sight of the wounded wayfarer who had fallen among thieves. Christ embraces our suffering, identifying with us to the point of death on a cross: "[he] loved me and gave himself for me" (Gal. 2:20), as Saint Paul puts it. This identification manifests our dignity. If Christ deems us worth suffering for, if "[we have been] bought with a price" (1 Cor. 6:20), then how great must our dignity be! Indeed, the contemplation of the Pierced One brings home to us how greatly the Father himself loves us: "He who did not spare his own Son but gave him up for us all, will he not also give us all things with him?" (Rom. 8:32). As John Paul II writes in his first encyclical: "The Cross on Calvary, through which Jesus Christ . . . 'leaves' this world, is also a fresh manifestation of the eternal fatherhood of God, who in him draws near again to humanity, to each human being" (*RH*, 9).

Christ's suffering, then, doesn't simply restore the language in which the body once spoke of original solitude and original unity in the same breath. Rather his suffering is the most eloquent "statement" of these original experiences that the body's language has ever uttered. Put more concretely, Christ's suffering flesh fulfills what we have called the "nuptial meaning of the body." Think of the words with which Christ institutes the Eucharist: "This is my body, which is given up for you." In pronouncing this simple sentence, Christ fulfills the language of the body, because his words enact the total gift of his own flesh that manifests the Father's love for the world. Christ achieves the will of the Father *as his Son*, precisely by giving himself up for the salvation of the Church as her *Bridegroom*: "For this reason the Father loves me, because I lay down my life that I may take it again . . . this charge I have received from my Father" (John 10:17–18). Christ, Son and Bridegroom, reveals and crowns by his bodily action both original solitude and original unity, both love for the Father and communion with his brothers. In *Reflections on Fatherhood*, Karol Wojtyla sings the praises of this "love that reveals the Father in the Son and in the Father, through the Son, gives birth to the Bridegroom. Father and Bridegroom: how much He strives for every human being—as for the greatest treasure, a unique good; as someone in love strives for his beloved: the Bridegroom and the Son" (*Ref Fath*, 368).

WE ARE THE FRUITS OF CHRIST'S LOVE

So far we've seen that Christ is the Son and Bridegroom who embodies the full revelation of love. This insight, important as it is, still leaves us with a question. After all, we're not Christ, and we fall far short of his perfection as Son and Bridegroom. How, then, do we come to share in his fulfillment of love? Or, as Adam puts it in *Reflections on Fatherhood*:

> Though I look at the Son with admiration, yet I cannot transform myself into Him. How full of human substance He is! He is the living denial of all loneliness. If I knew how to immerse myself in Him, if I knew how to implant myself in Him, I would find in myself the love that fills Him. (*Ref Fath*, 368)

In order to understand how Christ initiates us into his experience, we need to consider the role of the Holy Spirit, who transforms us into Christ's image of the Son and Bridegroom. In fact, Christ's own earthly actions all take place in the Spirit of love that unites him with the Father. Just as "fire from heaven" consumed men's sacrifices in the Old Testament, "[b]y analogy one can say that the Holy Spirit is the 'fire from heaven' which works in the depth of the mystery of the Cross. Proceeding from the Father, he directs toward the

Father the sacrifice of the Son, bringing it into the divine reality of the Trinitarian communion" (John Paul II, *Dominum et Vivificantem*, 41).

Christ communicates to us his Spirit on the day of Pentecost. This gift of the Spirit ushers us into the space of Christ's love and plunges us into the inner depth of his experience. The Holy Spirit, then, is the "communication of Christ" (as the great theologian of the early Church Saint Irenaeus of Lyons once put it).[10] John Paul II says in *The Jeweler's Shop*:

> The Bridegroom passes through so many streets,
> meeting so many different people.
> Passing, he touches the love
> that is in them. (*JS*, 55)

The Spirit touches "the love that is in man" by attuning our hearts and "the love that is in them" to the Heart of Jesus. As Pope Benedict XVI says: "The Spirit, in fact, is that interior power which harmonizes [the believers'] hearts with Christ's heart and moves them to love their brethren as Christ loved them, when he bent down to wash the feet of the disciples [cf. John 13:1–13] and above all when he gave his life for us" (cf. John 13:1, 15:13; *DCE*, 19).

A final point is that Jesus's gift of the Spirit contains an additional "message" for the spouses. It is as if Christ said to them: "beloved, you do not know how deeply you are mine, how much you belong to my love and my suffering—because to love means to give life through death; to love means to let gush a spring of the water of life into the depths of the soul, which burns or smolders, and cannot burn out" (*JS*, 64).

"To love means to let a spring of the water of life gush into the depths of the soul." As we have seen, love's inner dynamism tends to fruitfulness. But just as the love between spouses spills over into the generation of new life, the love Christ shares with us is fruitful of a new birth through the Holy Spirit. "We are the fruit [of Christ] in virtue of his . . . Passion," in the words of the early Church Father Ignatius of Antioch.[11] Or, as Mother exclaims in *Radiation of Fatherhood*: "My Bridegroom does not want to remain lonely in his death!" (*RF*, 363). No, he sends his Spirit from the Cross to re-create us as children of the Father. All that remains now is to accept the Spirit's invitation to transform our love into the image of Christ's love.

CHRIST IS THE PATH OF THE IMAGE

We saw in chapter 4 that the *imago Dei* is not just an image; it involves a process. First, we learn to be children and to accept our existence from the hands of God; then, by giving ourselves to one another in a loving spousal exchange, we answer the Father's love and become parents whose fruitfulness participates in the fecundity of God himself. The family is the natural habitat in which we live out the fullness of the divine image through the adventure of learning to be children, spouses, and parents.

In the present chapter we enrich this account of the divine image with a deeper understanding of Christ's identity as Son, Bridegroom, and Source of the fruitfulness of the Church. The awesome revelation of the love of God in Christ's life, we now see, proceeds along the ordinary path of our being children (Christ, the Son), spouses (Christ, the Bridegroom), and parents (Christ, fruitful in his self-gift)—and just so brings the human journey to its unexpected crowning in God. God's salvation is great because it is simple:

"And everything else will then turn out to be unimportant and inessential, except for this: father, child, and love. And then, looking at the simplest things, all of us will say: could we not have learned this long ago? Has this not always been embedded at the bottom of everything that is?" (*Ref Fath*, 368).

Christ reopens to us the path of love. Although the voice of concupiscence still whispers in our heart, Christ's love resounds even more ringingly, encouraging us to overcome the obstacles to true love: "And now there are two of us in the history of every man: I who conceive and bear loneliness" (loneliness, remember, was the bitter fruit of concupiscence), "and He [Christ] in whom loneliness disappears and children are born anew" (*RF*, 339). Our task in the next chapter is to consider how "loneliness disappears" in the new life of communion offered to the "children born anew."

CHAPTER 7

MATURING IN
THE FULLNESS
OF LOVE

THE OVERARCHING THEME OF JOHN PAUL II'S THEOLOGY
of the body is man's journey to the fullness of love. We could think
of John Paul's account of this journey as a modern-day retelling of
Dante's *Divine Comedy*. Even as a young man, Karol Wojtyla was
involved in a stage production of Dante's poem, which a friend of
his had adapted for the Rhapsodic Theater, an underground theater
group cofounded by the future pope during World War II. Translated into the clandestine ensemble's spare, intense performance style,
which relied almost solely on the spoken word, the *Divine Comedy*
became a representation of essential human experience. By the same
token, the thirteenth-century "story of the soul of Dante . . . who
goes through hell, purgatory, and heaven but goes through them on
earth, as a man who believes and loves"[1] is an apt illustration of the
journey of human existence that John Paul II maps out for us in his
theology of the body.

In order to grasp the force of Dante's portrait of our life's adventure, we need to remember that the poet's journey is directed toward
heaven. Each of the three parts of the *Divine Comedy* ends with the

word "star" or "stars," which stands for heaven (the Latin root of the word "desire," *desiderium*, originally meant an aspiration to the stars). Significantly, desire has a bodily side for Dante. After having suffered through the cleansing of purgatory, for instance, the poet is astonished to find that the weight of his body now propels him upward, instead of dragging him downward to the earth. Beatrice, the woman whom Dante loved on earth and who guides him through heaven, explains this marvel in this passage:

No more amazement should it bring to you
that you ascend, than if a mountain stream
should rumble rushing to the plains below.
But it would be a cause of just surprise
if, free of every bar, you should remain
like a still flame on earth, and not arise.[2]

Beatrice's image of the stream that rushes from the mountain's summit to its base brings us back to the starting point of our journey in this book. We saw in the introduction that man is much more than a stream that simply "goes with the flow" of its own current. True, man's body is subject to the law of gravity. But the human body also has a special "gravity" of its own: "My weight is my love," writes Saint Augustine, "wherever I am carried, my love is carrying me."[3] As Dante discovers on the threshold of heaven, the impetuous gravity of love is stronger than every obstacle that would hinder man's upward path to God.

Before following the trajectory of this upward flight any further, it will be helpful to review the stages of love's ascent that we traced in chapter 2. We saw there that the mutual attraction of man and woman, rooted in their bodies, draws the two out of themselves and into a covenant with each other. This movement consists of the gradual integration of the following four dimensions of human love.

The first dimension is the sensual impulse toward sexual pleasure. Far from being an end in itself, however, sensuality calls for integration on the second and higher level of love where feelings and emotions are at home. It's only on this second level, in fact, that man and woman begin to experience the world together. Yet even this second level is not a final resting place; it points in turn to a third dimension in love's ascent: the affirmation of the value of the person. This mutual yes is the golden key that finally liberates man and woman from themselves and frees them to love each other for his or her own sake.

Although to integrate this third dimension might look like the final stop on love's journey, a fourth level is still needed to cement and crown love's dynamic unfolding. It's true, of course, that the affirmation of the person is the bedrock on which man and woman are called to build up their stable communion of life. But you can't fully affirm another person unless you recognize his connection with God, the original Source of love and life. Indeed, to accept and love another person is already the first step on the way to loving God himself.

Dante is right, then. The gravitational pull of bodily love is truly a path to the "stars," a path whose inner dynamism aspires to communion with God. Nevertheless, it's not easy to follow the journey to its end. Even if love seems to promise us an ecstasy of happiness, its growth is hindered by many difficulties along the way. First of all, there is sin: The four dimensions of love we just mentioned have lost their original integration, and this disorder diminishes their utility as a compass for life's journey. Concupiscence binds man fast in the chains of his own loneliness. Furthermore, even if sin and concupiscence were removed from the picture, we would still have to acknowledge that we are mere creatures who by definition fall infinitely short of their Creator. How, then, can we entertain even the faintest hope of "reaching the stars"?

Fortunately, these difficulties need not cause us to despair. The good news, as we learned in chapter 6, is that Christ gives us a fresh start on the journey to love. Not only does he free us from our sins, but he himself is love's Way to God (see *DCE*, 1). The question we need to ponder now is this: How does Christ give love the boost it needs to reach the stars it longs for so ardently? Also how do we reconcile the four dimensions of love we listed just now—dimensions that are often at war within man's heart?

The Law in Man's Heart

A good place to begin our reflections on the ripening of love is John Paul II's discussion of Christ's dispute with the Pharisees concerning the Law of Moses. In order to understand this debate correctly, we need to rid ourselves of the prejudice that the Mosaic Law was merely a set of orders to be obeyed without love or understanding. On the contrary, Israel rejoiced in the Law and welcomed it as a precious gift that revealed the path of life and taught man how to love in truth. The essence of the Mosaic Law is love—love of God and love of neighbor—as Jesus himself stresses in the Gospels. Indeed, Christ himself did not come to abolish the Law, but to fulfill it (Matt. 5:17) with a gift of righteousness surpassing even the justice of those scrupulous Law keepers, the Scribes and Pharisees (Matt. 5:20).

The eighth chapter of John's Gospel illustrates how Jesus fulfills the Law. The Evangelist recounts that the Pharisees brought an adulteress before Jesus and asked him whether she should be stoned as Moses commanded (John 8). Jesus responds by bending down and drawing in the dust with his finger. Saint Augustine bases his commentary on this enigmatic gesture—which scholars still argue about today—on the observation that in ancient times God wrote the Law on tablets of stone. Just as God wrote the Law with his finger, Saint Augustine continues, Jesus rewrites it with his. But there is an important difference: Jesus does not write the New Law on stone but on the ground, which symbolizes the rich soil of the human heart that he tills and makes fruitful. Jesus fulfills the Law by writing it on our hearts. His grace empowers us to bear the fruit of righteousness in the same way that sunlight and water enable the soil to yield an abundant crop at harvest time.

The New Law begins its work of transformation in man's heart, which, as the Bible teaches, is the core of the human being: "The 'heart,' " John Paul II writes, "is the dimension of humanity with which the sense of the meaning of the human body, and the order of this sense, is directly linked" (*TOB*, 231).[4] The "meaning of the body," which John Paul speaks of in this text, is the capacity to express love. By the same logic, the heart is the meeting place where the four dimensions of love converge. The heart brings together sensuality, the emotions, and the affirmation of the person, and it is in the heart that these dimensions of love open of one accord to divine transcendence.

Jesus, we said a moment ago, fulfills the Law by writing it on the human heart. Since the heart is our center of unity, Christ thereby integrates all the dimensions of love within that center. The Law written in stone is already a law of love, but it is powerless to transform our desires and feelings into an expression of that love. By contrast, Jesus heals the heart, reorienting sensuality and emotion to true love of God and neighbor. The justice that surpasses the righteousness of the Scribes and Pharisees is the reattunement of our desires and feelings to the value of the person in light of his relation to God.

John Paul II, along with the whole Christian tradition, defines the integration of the heart's desires and feelings as a "virtue": the virtue of "purity" or "chastity," to be precise. Nowadays, chastity is often tarred with the brush of prudish negativity toward sex, but this is an unfortunate and unfair caricature. Real chastity has nothing to do with so-called "puritanism," but is a life-affirming self-mastery in love. Chastity is the fruit of Christ's gentle education of the heart, which gradually shapes the heart's desires and feelings into a reflection of true love for others.

VIRTUE AND THE ORDER OF LOVE

Before going on to discuss chastity, we should pause briefly to offer a few words in defense of virtue in general, a concept that is at least as thoroughly misunderstood as the virtue of purity in particular. Most of us probably associate virtue with rule keeping; being virtuous, we typically think, means "playing by the rules." Genuine virtue, by contrast, is not about the legalistic observance of rules, but about the kind of person you are. In a word, virtue is an interior quality, and its presence transforms us from the inside out into better people.

In order to understand how we become virtuous persons, we can think of the way a person is educated by the influence of good friends. A true friend does not sit in judgment on his fellows. Rather, he lifts them up; not by being patronizing and lecturing them, but just by being the kind of person he is and sharing with them his own life. True friends teach us by their very presence to reject evil and to embrace the good; they themselves embody the good for us as a living law that we can follow. As Saint Gregory of Nazianzus said of his friendship with Saint Basil, "if this is not too much for me to say, we were a rule and standard for each by which we learned the distinction between what was right and what was not."[5]

Friendship starts with affective union; a good friend shares our emotions and feelings. By the same token, his educative influence touches our emotional life on the inside. Consider the following illustration: If we scatter iron filings over a sheet of paper and place a magnet underneath, the tiny shavings regroup into a new pattern along the lines of force emanating from the magnet. In the same way, the love of our friends "magnetizes" our desires and affections, drawing all the feelings and movements of our hearts into a well-ordered pattern. Friendship integrates all the dimensions of our being and empowers us to become agents of our own interior integration in turn.

Saint Thomas Aquinas describes the virtues as the fruit of a friendship. Thomas's term for this friendship is "charity." Here is yet another misunderstood word. Whereas we nowadays tend to associate "charity" mainly with philanthropy on behalf of the "less fortunate," for Saint Thomas charity goes much deeper than donating money (important as that is). Charity, as Saint Thomas understands it, is actually a friendship with God that "has been poured into our hearts through the Holy Spirit which has been given to us" (Rom. 5:5). Charity, in its turn, is like a "mother" that gives birth to all the other virtues. Karol Wojtyla says in the same vein that charity is "a virtue, and the greatest of virtues" (*LR*, 74).

Long before Saint Thomas and John Paul II, Saint Augustine made a similar point about the four "cardinal virtues" of temperance, fortitude, justice, and prudence that, according to the sages of

Greece and Rome, are the hinges ("cardinal" comes from the Latin *cardo*, meaning "hinge") on which every other virtue turns. For Saint Augustine, even these four basic virtues are themselves expressions of love:

> For the fourfold division of virtue I regard as taken from four forms of love. For these four virtues ... I should have no hesitation in defining them: that temperance is love giving itself entirely to that which is loved; fortitude is love readily bearing all things for the sake of the loved object; justice is love serving only the loved object, and therefore ruling rightly; prudence is love distinguishing with sagacity between what hinders it and what helps it.[6]

The upshot of this traditional teaching about the primacy of charity is that we cannot even think about acquiring virtue—and virtue just means the integration of the various dimensions of the heart—unless we already stand within the magnetic field of true love. The gift of love has to come first and take us by surprise, otherwise we lack the wherewithal even to start the work of integrating our hearts. By the same token, every effort to attain virtue (if it's real virtue we are after) flows from love and strengthens it in turn. Striving for real virtue has nothing to do with egotistical perfectionism or self-realization; the true goal is a richer capacity to love and an enhanced ability to give ourselves to others.

The story of Adam Chmielowski, the main character of Wojtyla's play *Our God's Brother*, illustrates virtue's aspiration to love. Adam's search for an ideal beauty to inspire his work as a painter leads him in a totally unexpected direction. It is in his encounter with the poor and suffering where he discovers the call to real beauty. Capturing beauty on a canvas isn't enough, Adam realizes; he himself must be transformed into the image of love. As Adam struggles to answer this new call, his confessor advises him: "Let yourself be molded by love!" (*OGB*, 210). Virtue, Adam's story suggests, is nothing but the interior shape into which love molds us. Accordingly, the question we need to ask now is this: What is the love that fashions our lives into a reflection of its beauty?

FRIENDSHIP WITH CHRIST IN HIS SPIRIT

The previous chapter focused our attention on Christ, who is at once the Son of the Father and the Bridegroom of a new humanity. But Christ is also the Friend who shares with us his love for the Father and his fellow men. By imparting this gift to us, he empowers us to reconfigure our lives into a reflection of true beauty, as Adam Chmielowski realizes in *Our God's Brother*:

> You have toiled in every one of them.
> You are deadly tired.
> They have exhausted You.
> This is called Charity.
> But with all this You have remained beautiful.
> The most beautiful of the sons of men.
> Such beauty was never repeated again.
> Oh what a difficult beauty, how hard.
> Such beauty is called charity. (*OGB*, 227)

Picking up an insight from the previous section, we can add that it's the Holy Spirit, the love of Christ the Son and Bridegroom, who orders our hearts from within. The Spirit allows us to participate in Christ's life, in his obedience to the Father as the Son and in his love for his fellow men as the Bridegroom. The way in which Christ orders our hearts from the inside is by letting us enter into this love, who is the Spirit.

The Spirit's work is to mold our hearts into the shape of Christ's love. Think of the water formed from snow melting in the mountains. By itself, the snow is too pure for us to drink, for it lacks the mineral content our stomach needs to absorb it. The melted snow becomes ready to enter our system only when it flows down the mountain and, little by little, absorbs minerals from the rock that help our body retain the water. Similarly, we cannot drink directly from the fountain of God's love—the Holy Spirit. The water of the Spirit needs to pass first through Christ's earthly life, death, and Resurrection. Christ's mission is like a "filter" that adapts the water of the Spirit to our human experience, enabling us to assimilate it as nourishment for our journey in the Lord's footsteps. Having flowed down the mountain of Christ's life, the water of the Spirit enters into our spiritual bloodstream and gushes forth as righteousness from our hearts.

THE VIRTUE OF PURITY

So far, we've seen how Christ's love redeems the body by reshaping our hearts from the inside into a living enfleshment of divine life. The redemption of the body thus institutes a new measure of holiness. This new standard of sanctity is not a set of commandments, however, but according to Pope John Paul II, the presence of Christ's love in the Spirit, radiating outward from our hearts through every pore of our bodies: *"The redemption of the body* brings with it the establishment in Christ and for Christ of a new *measure of the holiness of the body.* Paul appeals precisely to this holiness when he writes in 1 Thessalonians that one should 'keep one's own body with holiness and reverence' " (*TOB*, 351).

The finger with which Christ traces the New Law in our heart is the Holy Spirit, who is the Lord's greatest gift to us (see Matt. 12:28 and Luke 11:20). As we just said, the Spirit fills our affections, indeed, our whole bodily existence, with Christ's love and molds us into his likeness as Son and Bridegroom. It goes without saying, of course, that the Spirit will not transform us without our free cooperation. Christ's friendship is not just a gift, it's also a task. "The mystery of the redemption of the body, carried out by Christ," writes John Paul II, is "a source of a particular moral duty which commits the Christian to purity" (*TOB*, 352). Having received Christ's love through the Spirit, we become free to act lovingly in our turn—just as the gift of inspiration (a word, be it noted, related etymologically to the word "spirit") enables the musician to create new works of music that bear the unmistakable stamp of his unique personality.

God has given us our bodies as a task of love. This means that our response to the Creator's gift must be expressed in our concrete bodily existence. We are called to attune our bodily feelings and emotions to the value of the person so that they help us discover and protect the truth of love. The redemption of the body according to the pope is the source of a new dignity, which by its very nature imposes a new obligation to live in accordance with its lofty demands:

> Through redemption, every man has received from God again, as it were, himself and his own body. Christ has imprinted new dignity on the human body—on the body of every man and ev-

ery woman, since in Christ the human body has been admitted, together with the soul, to union with the Person of the Son-Word. With this new dignity, through the redemption of the body, a new obligation arose at the same time. Paul writes of this concisely, but in an extremely moving way: "You were bought with a price" (1 Cor. 6:20). The fruit of redemption is the Holy Spirit, who dwells in man and in his body as in a temple. In this Gift, which sanctifies every man, the Christian receives himself again as a gift from God. (*TOB*, 350–51)

The "obligation" John Paul II speaks of in this passage is not a burdensome commandment, but a call to integrate the various dimensions of our life in love. Let's go back for a moment to the image of the magnet and the iron filings. When we enter through the Spirit into the sphere of Christ's love, the iron filings of our emotions and sentiments are drawn into a harmonious pattern. Far from suppressing our freedom, the Spirit enables us to integrate all the dimensions of our life in this pattern reflecting the magnetic field love generates in our hearts.

The integration of the body in response to love's call is the work of chastity or purity of heart. This virtue is not prudery, but an enhancement of the capacity to love. As John Paul II puts it with categorical succinctness: "Chastity can only be thought of in association with the virtue of love" (*LR*, 169).

The first *consequence* of purity is self-mastery. We could think of self-mastery as an attitude of vigilance that watches over the unity of the heart by preserving its rightly ordered love. This self-mastery, Saint Augustine writes in the *Confessions*, ensures that "we are collected together and brought to the unity from which we disintegrated into multiplicity."[7] This unity keeps our sensuality and feelings in the service of love's affirmation of the person for his own sake:

> Thus also only the chaste man and the chaste woman are capable of true love. For chastity frees their association, including their marital intercourse, from the tendency to use a person which is objectively incompatible with loving kindness, and by so freeing it introduces into their life together and their sexual relationship a special disposition to loving kindness. (*LR*, 171)

Purity entails vigilance, but vigilance is not the soul of the pure heart. If vigilance were the essence of purity, then this virtue would be a merely negative attitude that was always on the defensive. Vigilance is important, but it is just a consequence of purity, and it exists solely to protect the unity of love against potential disruptions. The fact is that you can't possess yourself unless you first receive yourself from another person. Moreover, the whole point of self-possession is to enable you to make a gift of yourself in return. Accordingly, the essence of purity lies in the desire to give ourselves entirely to the true beauty of another person, so that "[c]hastity is . . . above all the 'yes' of which certain 'no's' are the consequence" (*LR*, 170). To be pure means to be capable of loving with the true love that builds up the communion of persons: "The task of purity . . . is not only (and not so much) abstaining from 'unchastity' and from what leads to it, that is, abstaining from 'lustful passions,' but, at the same time, keeping one's body, and indirectly that of the other, in 'holiness and reverence'" (*TOB*, 343).

Purity of heart, then, is both self-possession or self-mastery, on the one hand, and attraction to love, or the desire to honor and serve beauty, on the other. It is in the words of Saint Augustine both "love keeping itself entire and incorrupt" and "love giving itself entirely to that which is loved."[8] For the goal of purity isn't our own isolated perfection, but an enhanced capacity to love others. Purity accordingly obliges man and woman to understand each other's emotions and to help each other integrate their feelings and desires. Far from being opposed to the art of love, as some people think, the Church knows that there can be no true art of love without purity's delicate vigor. The genuine *ars amatoria* is the ability to express love in our bodies by integrating our desires and feelings into the affirmation of God and neighbor: "Love consists in the thoroughgoing transformation of sympathy into friendship . . . This is where the 'art' of education in love, the true 'ars amandi' comes into its own" (*LR*, 93).

The pope does not hesitate to call on spouses to pursue this "transformation of sympathy into friendship" even in their erotic love. Purity is the key to that affectionate friendship without which erotic love between man and woman quickly loses its beauty and joy. Purity frees us to follow our desires, but first it transforms them into a loving response to the value of the person. Only then does the erotic shine with the light of love: "What is worthy of the human 'heart' is that the form of the 'erotic' is at the same time the form of ethos, that is, of that which is 'ethical' " (*TOB*, 318).

Purity, to repeat what we said just now, is essentially positive, not negative. It fosters the spouses' capacity to see the world from each other's point of view. It empowers them to help each other integrate desire and emotion into love. By the same token, the virtue of purity is anything but mere custom or routine. Routine means uninvolvement; it means sleepwalking through our lives without seizing the new gift love offers us moment by moment. Virtue, by contrast, is not some autopilot of the soul but the ability to live intensely as great lovers. This doesn't mean, of course, that virtue is a permanent "high." The point is simply that virtue is an active readiness to see love shining through the body even in its most humdrum guise. Virtue is the freedom to respond fruitfully to the revelation of love "in sickness and in health, for better and for worse."

John Paul II calls virtue the key to *true* spontaneity. Notice the adjective "true." There is a crucial difference between the chaotic spontaneity of "anything goes" and the real spontaneity that flows from the integration of the body's feelings and desires into the order of love. If the patient labor required for such genuine spontaneity sounds like a wet blanket to smother joy, ask yourself this: Which would you rather be—a child who grabs a piece of paper and doodles any odd thing or a skilled artist who takes the same piece of paper and draws a masterpiece on it?

The Danish philosopher Søren Kierkegaard captured what we've been trying to say here in the brilliant title he gave to one of his books: *Purity of Heart Is to Will One Thing*.⁹ Purity does not truncate; it integrates, uniting all the movements, desires, and feelings of the heart in true love of God and neighbor. In the *Divine Comedy*, Virgil leaves Dante at the gates of heaven with the assurance that he no longer needs a guide, because the poet's own desire, healed and integrated, is now guide enough:

> I've led you here by strength of mind, and art;
> take your own pleasure for your leader now.
> You've left the steep and narrow ways behind . . .
> No longer wait for what I do or say.
> Your judgment now is free and whole and true;
> to fail to follow its will would be to stray.
> Lord of yourself I crown and mitre you.¹⁰

THE GIFT OF PIETY

Our survey of John Paul II's teaching about the virtue of purity would be incomplete if we left out his reflections on the gift of piety, which he regards as the consummation of chastity. Piety, one of the seven "gifts of the Holy Spirit" identified by Catholic tradition, gives purity what we might call a "charismatic" depth. The word "charismatic," from the Greek *charis*, meaning "grace," underscores that purity is not so much a result of human effort as it is a fruit of the Spirit's work in us. Chastity, like all the virtues, starts with a gift of love, and it can be fulfilled only by another gift that perfects the first. Progress in virtue bestows self-mastery, but—contrary to what we might think—self-mastery grows in proportion to our awareness of how continually we stand in need of a gift that only another can bestow. Our perfection is based on a gift from above, even though this gift arouses and includes our own effort to attain the ideal. The ultimate stage of our journey is God himself, but we cannot reach him unless he comes down to lift us up. After having exclaimed, "My weight is my love," Saint Augustine continues: "By your gift we are set on fire and carried upwards: we grow red hot and ascend . . . Lit by your fire, your good fire, we grow red-hot and . . . move upwards."[11] What Saint Augustine is telling us is that the Holy Spirit—God's fire—is meant to become the weight by which our love carries us upward to God.

It's crucial to keep in mind that piety isn't simply a relationship between "me and God." John Paul II identifies piety with the awareness of God's presence in human love, an awareness that flourishes in the atmosphere of the family and the relationships between man and woman, parent and child that make up the life of the household. Piety relates us to God as the source and sustainer of the love between man and woman, parent and child: "This gift sustains and develops in the spouses a singular sensibility for all that in their vocation and shared life carries the sign of the mystery of creation and redemption: for all that is a created reflection of God's wisdom and love" (*TOB*, 654).[12] Piety opens our eyes, then, to the relation to God built into human love itself; it is a perception of the sacredness of God's image in other persons, and it spills over into a reverence for our own body as well. The body isn't only a home in which the individual encounters the world, or even just the vehicle of communion between man and woman. Rather, from the first moment of its existence, the body is called to become a temple:

> Purity as a virtue . . . allied with the gift of piety as a fruit of the Holy Spirit's indwelling in the "temple" of the body, causes in the body such a fullness of dignity in interpersonal relations that *God himself is thereby glorified*. Purity is the glory of the human body before God. It is the glory of God in the human body, through which masculinity and femininity are manifested. (*TOB*, 353)

If the body is a temple, it calls for reverence. Reverence, however, demands a crucial ingredient of piety: humility, the refusal of that prideful absolutization of our own feelings that Karol Wojtyla describes in a passage of *The Jeweler's Shop* we quoted earlier: "they do not try to connect that love with the Love that has such [an absolute dimension]. They do not even feel the need, blinded as they are not so much by the force of their emotion as by lack of humility. They lack humility towards what love must be in its true essence" (*JS*, 88).

Fortunately for us, humility is not foreign to the body. On the contrary, the body, created to be a sign of transcendence, is by that very fact naturally "humble." Here is Wojtyla's more technical account of the body's native humility in *Love and Responsibility*:

> Humility is the proper attitude towards all true greatness, including one's own greatness as a human being, but above all towards the greatness which is not oneself, which is beyond one's self. The human body must be "humble" in face of the greatness represented by the person: for in the person resides the true and definitive greatness of man. Furthermore, the human body must "humble itself" in face of the magnitude represented by love . . . The body must also show humility in face of human happiness. (*LR*, 172)

The gift of piety remedies pride, then, by reawakening us to the humility of the body. When we accept this humility, we fulfill the body's vocation, which is nothing less than to manifest the Source of love whom Jesus taught us to call "Father."

The chaste humility Wojtyla sees radiating from the body finds a powerful illustration in the *Divine Comedy*. On reaching the entrance to purgatory, the poet is astonished by the beauty of a lifelike sculpture of the Annunciation carved by the hand of God himself.[13] Mary's whole pose is so expressive that Dante can almost hear her assenting to the Incarnation, despite the fact that the statue itself does not speak. Even without words, Mary is the purest expression of the love for God and neighbor in which chastity rises exultantly to its crowning perfection. All she has to do in order to radiate this love is be the fully alive, because Spirit-filled, body that she is.

Dante's vivid image indicates the task awaiting us in the third part of this book, to which we now turn. Our discussion in what follows will focus on the family's mission to shine in the midst of the world with the splendor of the redeemed body. In particular, we will consider how man and woman embody the transparency of love either in marriage (chapter 8) or consecrated virginity (chapter 9), and so build up both the Church and human society (chapter 10). As we set out on this final stage of our voyage, it's reassuring to know that everyone who climbs the mountain of purgatory in Dante's *Comedy*— a symbol for him of the Christian journey of purification—stands under the protecting hand of Mary, who educates us on the freedom of her yes to the fulfillment of the divine plan.

PART III

THE BEAUTY
OF LOVE:
THE SPLENDOR
OF THE
BODY

CHAPTER 8

LOVING WITH THE LOVE OF CHRIST: THE SACRAMENT OF MARRIAGE

THE FIRST ACT OF *THE JEWELER'S SHOP*, WHICH TELLS THE story of Andrew and Teresa, culminates in the young couple's purchase of wedding rings. "Teresa, do you want to be the companion of my life?" Andrew asks his bride-to-be. Teresa answers "Yes," and the two immediately make their way to the Jeweler's shop to look for their wedding bands. As Andrew later recalls:

> The rings in the window
> appealed to us with a strange force.
> Now they are just artifacts of precious metal
> but it will be so only until that moment
> when I put one of them on Teresa's finger,
> and she puts the other on mine.
> From then on they will mark our fate. (*JS*, 33–34)

It is surely not accidental that the first act of the *The Jeweler's Shop* is entitled "The Signals." Wedding rings figure prominently in the drama of Teresa and Andrew because they are signals or signs of the sacrament of marriage, which binds man and woman together in a lifelong, fruitful communion of love. Wedding rings symbolize the marriage bond that, as Andrew says in the soliloquy we just quoted, is endowed with a "strange force." In the present chapter our exploration of this matrimonial bond aims to show how the indissolubility and fruitfulness of marriage fulfill and crown the dynamism of the love we've watched unfolding in this book.

THE SIGN OF THE BODY

A key idea we've looked at in this book is that the body speaks a language. What this language tells us is that the human person is no solitary island, but receives his or her identity from relationship— with the world, with others, and with God. Ultimately, the body's language echoes the voice of transcendence inviting us to venture out of ourselves in response to the call to love. At the same time, the body provides the grammar for this response. The body isn't dumb flesh, mere "meat," as it were, but a significant and beautiful pattern that gives our love the shape and structure it needs in order to find its true face as self-gift.

The body gives love a threefold pattern. First of all, the body is *filial*, because it represents man's solitude before God and man's openness toward Him; the body is man's meeting place with God the Father. At the same time, the body is *nuptial*, because the body's very identity as male or female is a vocation to become a spouse and to journey toward the Giver from whom man and woman receive themselves and each other as a gift. Finally, the body has a *procreative* meaning, inasmuch as the union of the spouses finds its proper completion in openness to the Creator's gift of fruitfulness.

The body, then, is a call to be a child, a spouse, and a parent and a pathway for living out this call. Or else we could think of the three-fold pattern of childhood, spousehood, and parenthood as a set of instructions for reflecting the *imago Dei* in our lives. This suggests a further crucial point: If we define a "sacrament" as the visible embodiment of an invisible reality, then we can call our journey along love's threefold path a *"sacrament of creation."* As we live out this journey, we visibly incarnate the image of the invisible God in the world. Although this sacrament of creation isn't one of the Church's official seven sacraments, it is the preliminary sketch of what Christian marriage (which *is* one of the official seven) fully fleshes out before our eyes in living color. Since this statement is the key to understanding the Church's teaching about the indissolubility and fruitfulness of married love, we'll need to spend some time exploring it in the next section.

THE NEW MEASURE OF LOVE

We know from the second part of this book that Christ's bodily life, death, and Resurrection fully reveal God's love for man and perfectly flesh out man's response to that love. Christ is the Son and Bridegroom who walks the path of filial, spousal, and parental love and brings this threefold pattern to fulfillment. Christ doesn't simply repeat the old pattern; he enriches it with a new substance: his eternal relationship to the Father in the Holy Spirit. It's important to stress that Christ completes this process of enrichment by sending the Holy Spirit to vivify us. The Spirit, in turn, gives us life by fashioning us into the Church. For the Church is not a merely human invention; as Saint Paul reminds us toward the end of the first chapter of his Letter to the Ephesians, the Church is the living body of Christ, "the fullness of him who fills all in all" (Eph. 1:23). Familiarity with the phrase "body of Christ" has perhaps dulled our ears to the astounding claim Paul is making in this passage: It is in a body, the body of Christ, the apostle is telling us, that God's love is fully manifested in the world.

Later on in Ephesians, Paul illustrates Christ's relation to his body, the Church, in light of spousal love. He begins by recalling the teaching in Genesis that marriage brings about a one-flesh union between male and female: "a man leaves his father and mother and cleaves to his wife, and they become one flesh" (Gen. 2:24). Paul then goes on to apply the idea of one-flesh union to Christ and the Church: "This mystery is a profound one, and I am saying that it refers to Christ and the Church" (Eph. 5:32). Note that Paul's use of the word "mystery" comes very close to what we have defined above as a "sacrament." By "mystery," in fact, Paul means the visible embodiment of the Father's invisible love for man—a love that was hidden from all eternity, but that God has now fully manifested in Christ's life, death, and Resurrection. Paul's intention is clear: He is taking the sacrament of creation, which already reveals God's love, and showing how it gets fulfilled in a higher *sacrament of redemption*, which completes the revelation of God's love in the one-flesh union between Christ and the Church.

We usually think of time as an arrow flying irreversibly out of the past and into the future. Placed on this standard human time line, Christ's coming looks like just another link in a long chain of historical events stretching back to Adam and Eve. In the Letter to the Ephesians, Paul invites us to look at things the other way around. From God's point of view, Paul is telling us, Christ's coming is not some random event that happened to occur two thousand years ago.

For Christ is at the origin of all that exists and he brings the whole of creation to fulfillment. By the same token, Adam and Eve's one-flesh union may come first on *our* time line, but on *God's* time line it's Christ and his Church who come first. From God's point of view, in other words, the sacrament of creation gets its existence and meaning from the sacrament of redemption that Christ establishes by his own marriage to the Church. John Paul writes:

> The reality of the creation of man was already permeated by the perennial election of man in Christ: called to holiness through the grace of adoption as sons ... This supernatural endowment ... was brought about precisely out of regard for him, that one and only Beloved, while chronologically anticipating his coming in the body. (*TOB*, 505)

On our earthly time line, marriage appears long before Christ's coming. On God's time line, however, Christ's coming is the very raison d'être of marriage in the first place: Christ, after all, is none other than the eternal Son who is sent as Bridegroom to bring all of creation into communion with the Father. The universal institution of marriage, which goes back to creation, exists for the Christian sacrament of marriage, which Christ founds through his life, death, and Resurrection. Let's try to delve more deeply into the relationship between these two phases of matrimony, which we'll call "natural marriage" and "Christian marriage," respectively.

Natural marriage, as we just noted, goes back to the Garden of Eden (on our time line), even though God established it for the sake of Christ, in whom the world was created (on the divine time line). We know from earlier chapters that the Fall introduced a wound into Adam and Eve's one-flesh union. Fortunately, since natural marriage was created in Christ, he has the power to restore it to its former glory. Accordingly, the first task of Christian marriage is to recover the *sacrament of creation* once broken by sin. Nevertheless, Christ not only retrieves the ruptured harmony of the beginning; he brings natural marriage to fulfillment in his own one-flesh union with the Church. By the same token, Christian marriage doesn't just repair the original sacrament of creation; it raises that sacrament to new life within the *sacrament of redemption* that embodies the Bridegroom's love for the Church brought to perfection by his death on the Cross. Note that the sacrament of redemption doesn't do away with the threefold pattern of filial, nuptial, and procreative love, but completes it precisely by making it a vehicle for communicating Trinitarian life. The sacrament of redemption fulfills the body's destiny—which is at once filial, nuptial, and procreative—to manifest divine love in the world.

In a nutshell, Christian marriage is the fulfillment of natural marriage, which Christ completes by transforming the sacrament of creation (which, to repeat, consists in the threefold pattern of being a child, a spouse, a parent) into a visible embodiment of his love for the Church. By the same token, the life, death, and Resurrection of Jesus Christ incarnate a new measure of conjugal love. Christian spouses are called to love each other according to the mystery of Christ, "out of reverence for Christ" (Eph. 5:21). They are to become a living sign of the love between Christ and the Church:

> Husbands, love your wives, as Christ loved the church and gave
> himself up for her, that he might sanctify her, having cleansed
> her by the washing of water with the word, that he might pre-
> sent the church to himself in splendor, without spot or wrinkle

or any such thing, that she might be holy and without blemish. (Eph. 5:25–27)

The task to which Paul calls Christian spouses may sound daunting or even impossible. This impression fades, however, when we recall that Christ doesn't leave Christian spouses to their own devices; he shares with them the love that actuated his whole life as Son and Bridegroom, from his conception to his self-gift for the Church on the Cross. Moreover, the love Christ shares with the Christian couple is not a thing (like an impersonal "energy") but a person—the Holy Spirit, whom the risen Lord breathes on the spouses to purify their human love and bring it to fulfillment. Christian couples needn't despair of living up to the Gospel's new measure of marital love, then, because the gift of the Spirit brings their human love to the fullness of *conjugal charity*:

> The Spirit which the Lord pours forth gives a new heart, and renders man and woman capable of loving one another as Christ has loved us. Conjugal love reaches that fullness to which it is interiorly ordained, conjugal charity, which is the proper and specific way in which the spouses participate in and are called to live the very charity of Christ who gave Himself on the Cross. (*Familiaris Consortio*, 13)

The charity given by God is called "conjugal" in this context because marital life is the setting in which spouses are called to embody this charity. Through the gift of his Spirit, Christ enables man and wife to communicate his own divine love to each other precisely in their own one-flesh union. As the early Church Father Tertullian says, "[T]hey are both brethren and both fellow-servants; there is no separation between them in spirit or flesh; in fact they are truly two in one flesh and where the flesh is one, one is the spirit."[1] The Spirit transforms the couple's bodily union, indeed, their whole communion of life, into a sign of God's presence in their love. Christian marriage is a shared life in the Spirit, and it breathes the rich atmosphere created by the virtue of purity and the gift of piety:

> Those who unite with each other as spouses according to the eternal divine plan so as to become in some sense "one flesh" are in turn called by the sacrament to a life "according to the Spirit," such that this life corresponds to the "gift" received in the sacrament. In virtue of this "gift," by leading a life as spouses "according to the Spirit," they are able to discover the particular gratuitous gift in which they have come to share ... [L]ife "according to the Spirit" (or the grace of the sacrament of Marriage) allows man and woman to find the true freedom of the gift together with the awareness of the spousal meaning of the body in its masculinity and femininity. (*TOB*, 522–23)

The Christian couple's shared life in the Spirit enables them to be faithful to each other forever. The Spirit also opens them to the gift and task of procreating and educating children. We'll ponder these two essential and interrelated dimensions of Christian married love in the following sections of this chapter.

FAITHFULNESS FOREVER

Our first topic is fidelity, which Christian marriage seals in an indissoluble, lifelong commitment. John Paul II rejected the widespread prejudice that such lifelong faithfulness is an enemy of human love. The pope stressed marital fidelity precisely because he valued it as one of the two chief ways in which Christian marriage fulfills and crowns the sacrament of creation (the other being fruitfulness, on which more anon). John Paul II felt, in other words, that lovers certify their "fluency" in the language of the body precisely by pronouncing the yes of eternal fidelity:

> The words, "I take you as my wife / as my husband," bear within themselves precisely that perennial and ever unique and unrepeatable "language of the body," and they place it at the same time in the context of the communion of persons. "I promise to be faithful to you always, in joy and in sorrow, in sickness and in health, and to love you and honor you all the days of my life." (*TOB*, 103:5)

If we're honest with ourselves, we have to admit that John Paul's ringing affirmation of the undying fidelity of spousal love immediately runs up against two major stumbling blocks in our minds. On the one hand, we doubt whether it's really possible to commit to another human being a future that we ourselves do not yet possess. On the other hand, we fear that the act of binding ourselves to another person forever will rob us of our freedom. In this section, we'll explore how the rooting of spousal love in God requires and enables lifelong fidelity even in natural marriage. This exploration will set the stage for the next section, where we'll reflect on spousal fidelity in the context of Christian matrimony.

George Bernard Shaw nicely sums up the first of the two difficulties mentioned above. Marriage, writes Shaw with his characteristic wit, brings together two people "under the influence of the most violent, most insane, most delusive, and most transient of passions. They are required to swear that they will remain in that excited, abnormal, and exhausting condition continuously until death do them part."[2]

Put in less poetic terms, the problem Shaw formulates for us boils down to this: Since I'm not the master of my own future, how can I promise that I will never fall out of love with my potential spouse? Our earlier discussion of the four dimensions of love (see chapter 2) gives us the key to answering this difficulty. Marriage is *not*, as Shaw supposes, based only on feelings, which admittedly come and go. Marriage ultimately rests on the bedrock affirmation of the value of the person. Our emotions are a promise of happiness, but it is the maturity of love that assures us of its viability. For love's maturation integrates our sensual desire and feelings and attunes them to the eternal value of the one we love. Once this attunement is mature enough, potential spouses are ready to say "I do" and to consummate their consent through conjugal union. They are ready to say "forever," because they have learned to affirm each other's ultimate dignity as persons, not just with their minds, but also with their senses and emotions.

The force of Shaw's objection further dissipates when we realize that spouses don't have to muster up eternal love on their own. They can love each other with the requisite intensity of commitment because God has loved them first. To love means to participate in a transcendent reality that encompasses the lovers themselves; it means to trust in the Source of love that is God himself. By the same token, when the spouses draw their love from this source, they needn't base their promise of fidelity on their own strength alone; they can build on the greater love that embraces them.

In *The Jeweler's Shop* Karol Wojtyla gives poetic expression to the binding force of the greater Love that sustains marriage. Just as Andrew and Teresa's wedding rings are forged by the Jeweler, God's love backs up married love with the weight of God's own eternal being. In other words, the freedom to commit forever is based on a love that precedes us and carries us beyond our expectations. Supported by this love, the spouses find the courage to overcome their anxiety and doubt in the face of an uncertain future they can't control:

> *Andrew:* I had the feeling that he [the Jeweler] was seeking our hearts with his eyes and delving into our past. Does he encompass the future too? The expression of his eyes combined warmth with determination. The future for us remains an unknown quantity, which we now accept without anxiety. Love has overcome anxiety. The future depends on love.
> *Teresa:* The future depends on love. (*JS*, 42–43)

The wedding rings that betoken the marital covenant aren't just a sign of the spouses' intention to stay together; they also signify the transcendent reality that sustains their love and reinforces their unity. Having grasped this crucial point, we are now ready to tackle the second difficulty, which arises from our fear that committing ourselves "forever" robs us of our freedom. This fear reflects an impoverished conception of liberty that wrongly separates freedom from love. The truth is that real freedom is a response to love's invitation to partake of the new life it offers us. Benedict XVI makes the same point in terms of gift:

> [T]he greatest expression of freedom is not the search for pleasure without ever coming to a real decision; this apparent, permanent openness seems to be the realization of freedom, but it is not true. The true expression of freedom is the capacity to choose a definitive gift in which freedom, in being given, is fully rediscovered.[3]

The objection that lifelong fidelity enslaves us misses the point. Admittedly, being free does involve possessing your future in some sense. Nevertheless, mastering your future doesn't mean anxiously protecting it from commitment. In fact, the objection gets the true situation completely backward: It's actually only when you give your future to another that you truly possess it. For it's only then that your love—and your beloved's—are lifted up into a bond whose durability is guaranteed by nothing less than the Creator's indestructible power over every possible future contingency.

What enslaves us, then, is not commitment but the anxious fear of it. This fear hinders our capacity to entrust our future to our beloved (and with him or her to God)—and it is this capacity that lies at the core of real liberty. Think of a party of mountain climbers tethered together at the waist. The rope is not an obstacle to their freedom but an assurance that their potential missteps won't be fatal. Without the rope—without the bond of commitment—the climbers aren't free but wander aimlessly with no one to warn them away from the abyss. Absent the bond of commitment, what we get is not freedom but a "free fall" into self-destruction. Moreover, just as the rope hangs from the waist of a seasoned guide who is intimately acquainted with the terrain, the bond that unites the spouses is forged by God himself, who not only knows the way to happiness, but created the path to fulfillment in the first place. Far from rigidly constraining a man's and a woman's freedom of movement, the bond of marital fidelity liberates them for love's journey toward each other and toward their final goal: "We are secretly growing into one / because of these two rings," as Andrew says in *The Jeweler's Shop* (*JS*, 34).

CHRISTIAN FIDELITY

So far we've explored the indestructibility (or "indissolubility," to use the technical terminology) of the bond uniting a man and a woman in natural marriage. Rooted in the love of the Creator, spousal communion flowers in a lifetime commitment within the sacrament of creation. In short, the very nature of human love calls for a bond of lifelong fidelity. Having examined the indissolubility that is already integral to natural marriage, we now turn to consider how Christian marriage strengthens that bond beyond all human expectations.

Let's start from the universal human experience that love is risky: What if the beloved refuses our gift? What if he or she does not requite our love? Haunted by these questions, we hesitate to make the first move and back away from giving without expecting anything in return. Or, if we are already in a marriage wounded by our partner's unfaithfulness, we lack the courage to forgive, hampered as we are by our fear that the beloved will despise our offer of reconciliation and perhaps relapse into infidelity. Clearly, if each spouse, held back by the fear of taking the first step, simply waits for the other to act, mutual love will never be restored. *Someone* has to make the first move—but how does he or she summon up the resolve to offer forgiveness in the face of potential rejection?

The Christian answer to this difficulty is based on the fact that Jesus loved *both* spouses from the Cross, where he gave himself to the very sinners who hated him and rejected his gift (and that means all of us). Jesus, then, is the "Someone" who is always ready to make the first move; indeed, he is the one who has already fully assumed the risk of love. Christ's love, which enfolds us in its embrace even before we perform even the smallest act of love on our own, emboldens us to expose ourselves to the risk of loving. The firm assurance of his love gives us the confidence that, even if the beloved refuses our gift, no gesture of forgiveness on our part will remain unanswered. On the contrary, Christ is always ready to accept our small tokens of love and to make them fruitful. Christ's self-gift on the Cross (which is his wedding with the Church) is an inexhaustible treasury of strength from which Christian spouses can draw to renew their mutual love. The fullness of the Lord's self-gift empowers them to take the first step toward reconciliation in the hope that their covenant will continue to grow.

The upshot of what we've just said is this: The mutual love of Christian spouses is enfolded within Christ's love, which reinforces the bond of fidelity that is already an integral part of natural marriage. Indeed, by lifting human love into his relationship with the Church, Christ the Bridegroom transforms that love's innate promise of eternity into an expression of *his* total yes of unconditional faithfulness to his Bride. In exchanging their marriage vows, the spouses receive the Holy Spirit, who seals their mutual self-giving within the indestructible, or indissoluble, love between Christ and the Church.

Just as the unbreakable bond of natural marriage is rooted in the Creator's love, the indissolubility of Christian marriage (which reinforces the bond of natural marriage) is rooted in the love of Christ. The husband and wife share in the indestructible union between Christ and the Church, which is the real basis of their fidelity.

This doesn't mean, of course, that the sacrament of matrimony magically transforms the spouses into superheroes incapable of rejection, betrayal, or infidelity. Rather the durability of their marriage bond is rooted in Christ's unshakable love. It's not that Christian spouses don't have to work through difficulties together; but they can base their own halting efforts on Christ's inexhaustible fidelity, which he holds unfailingly ready for them in the sacraments (especially the Eucharist and confession). Rooted in Christ, the spouses never need despair of being able to love each other with his love, no matter what happens. For Christ's love is never shaken, nor does it draw back even in the face of indifference and rejection. The Lord remains faithful even to the point of crucifixion. Christ's love—which he shares with spouses—is an irresistible force that enables us to forgive and to give our life for our enemies. It is a love that "bears all things, believes all things, hopes all things, endures all things." It is a love that "never ends" (see 1 Cor. 13:7–8) and that therefore empowers us for unfailing fidelity in our turn.

THE GIFT OF NEW LIFE

Love between man and woman naturally seeks the lifelong, mutual commitment of marriage. This aspiration to fidelity, which already characterizes natural marriage, finds its fulfillment when Christ seals human love forever within the indestructible bond uniting him with his Church. Christian marriage expresses this indissoluble mutual commitment of Christ and the Church. It's crucial to stress that, in saying "forever" to each other through the conjugal embrace, Christian spouses also say yes to new life. The fidelity of married love is inseparable from openness to new life. For the same reason, the conjugal act not only expresses the union between the spouses but also signifies their acceptance of the gift of fruitfulness (should it be granted).

To understand this fruitfulness of marriage, we need to reflect on the crucial distinction between a *fruit* and a *product*. Whereas a product is the end result of a calculated and deliberate effort to transform the world by our own innate powers, the generation of a fruit always exceeds our native capabilities, and so is never completely subject to our choice or calculation. A product (assuming we do the job well) is more or less exactly what we want it to be, but a fruit is a surprise that is always different from, and better than, anything we could have hoped for.

The superabundant, or overflowing, quality of the fruit suggests a further crucial point: We can bear fruit only because we participate in a greater reality that transcends us and our innate capabilities—just as a tree is fruitful only if it's planted in fertile ground and receives plenty of sunlight and rain from heaven. In the same way, the conjugal union bears fruit only because it is rooted in God and shares in his creative power. Whereas fruitfulness of one kind or another characterizes every act of love between the spouses, marital love attains its greatest fruitfulness through that share in God's communication of the gift of new life known as procreation. Meditating on the link between conjugal union and openness to new life (between sex and procreation), John Paul II writes:

Into this truth of the sign, and consequently into the ethos of conjugal conduct, there is inserted, in a future-related perspective, *procreative meaning of the body*, that is, fatherhood and motherhood ... To the question, "Are you ready to accept children lovingly from God and bring them up according to the Law of Christ and his Church?" the man and the woman answer, "Yes." (*TOB*, 541–42)

Even at the level of natural marriage, then, the spouses' union is always enfolded within a greater unity that transcends them. In fact, their union with each other is itself a form of communion with the very Source of life. What, then, is the sign that conjugal love lives and moves and has its being within the Source? It is the fact that the child is a fruit that exceeds the spouses' innate ability to plan or produce. Since the child ultimately comes from a greater love that both embraces and transcends the parents, he or she is *not a thing to be produced, but a gift to be received*. Parents can never claim to be the owners of their children, because children are never simply the result of some decision on their part. The cry of the first woman—"I have gotten a man with the help of the LORD" (Gen. 4:1)—beautifully sums up this essential truth about procreation. As the mother of the Maccabean martyrs says to one of her sons: "I do not know how you came into being in my womb. It was not I who gave you life and breath, nor I who set in order the elements within each of you" (2 Macc. 7:22).

IN VITRO FERTILIZATION

Our ringing affirmation of the fruitfulness of conjugal love raises a question about spouses who are physically unable to have children. Understandably, some infertile couples are tempted to resort to techniques of artificial reproduction such as in vitro fertilization. Everyone knows that the Church frowns on such methods, but most people don't know the real reason why. It isn't that the Church is insensitive to the pain infertile couples experience. On the contrary, the Church rejects techniques such as in vitro fertilization precisely because it knows that these methods don't heal the wound of infertility, but only deepen it further. This statement requires some explanation.

The physical fruitfulness of conjugal union, we said, is rooted in a sphere that encompasses and transcends the love of the spouses. Another way of making the same point is to say that conjugal union is a language that is not invented by the spouses but that expresses the intentions of the divine Source of love and life. What does this language say? One of its main messages is this: The child resulting from conjugal union ultimately derives his or her existence from God's presence within the spouses' love; the spouses themselves are never the first origin of new life, but they share in God's work of communicating it. In a word, the very logic of conjugal union brings home to spouses (or should bring home to them) that the child is not a product. No, the child is a fruit that parents are called to welcome as a surprising gift beyond all deliberation and calculation.

Admittedly, people often talk about "deciding to have a child." A bit of reflection suffices, however, to show that this expression, if taken literally, is dangerously misleading. Parents may want to conceive a child, but the actual generation of a new life remains beyond their direct control. The fundamental decision spouses have to make is to love each other with full respect for the truth of conjugal love—which includes the openness to receive children (if they should come) as a gift.

We now see what is wrong with in vitro fertilization: It introduces into the generation of children a logic different from, and foreign to, the logic of gift. In vitro fertilization and similar techniques proceed as if the child resulted solely from the calculated decision of his or her parents. Such methods send the message—and incline doctors and parents to act accordingly—that the child is more a product to be chosen than a gift to be welcomed as the surprising fruit of a union of love. In vitro fertilization and allied procedures attempt to transform the generation of new life into a technique of manufacture. It goes without saying that this same logic inevitably blurs the connection between the child and the divine source of his or her life. In vitro fertilization disposes us to forget that the child is a mystery to be reverenced, and to treat him or her instead as an object to be manipulated.

What we've said suggests a further, related problem with in vitro fertilization: Since the procedure inclines parents to think of themselves as the sole originators of the new life they beget, they saddle themselves with an unbearable responsibility. After all, how could a mere human being guarantee the future happiness of his or her child? How could any parent redress the complaint of a child who exclaimed, Job-like, "Let the day perish wherein I was born" (Job 3:3)? Conversely, it's only when parents receive their child as the fruit of God's presence in their conjugal love that they can entrust his future to the Source from which he came. Openness to receive the child as a gift from God frees parents from the burden of total responsibility for his entire existence.

Let's be clear: Nothing we've said is meant to deny the real suffering endured by infertile couples. Our aim is to reassure such couples that they needn't despair of becoming fruitful in a different, though no less real, way. Indeed, the key to fruitfulness is the acceptance of the soil in which both partners are rooted: the love of God that sustains their relationship. If childless couples remain in communion with the Source of love and life, they can rest assured that their union—and even their suffering—will always be fruitful in a myriad of different ways. Hospitality, work in the community, or perhaps the adoption of children are just some of the ways in which childless couples can experience the gift of genuine fruitfulness and share it with others.

EDUCATION IN LOVE

The parents' mission is not over when their child is born. Once the fruit of their love has come into the world, it still needs to grow and be educated from within this same love.[4] This reflection suggests one reason that men and women are called to play different, but equally necessary, roles in the education of the child. Karol Wojtyla summarizes these complementary roles in *Radiation of Fatherhood*: "a woman knows infinitely more about giving birth than a man. She knows it particularly through the suffering that accompanies childbearing. Still, motherhood is an expression of fatherhood. It must always go back to the father to take from him all that it expresses" (*RF*, 341).

The first point Wojtyla makes in this passage is that a woman's connection with new life is internal both to her physiognomy and to the lived experience of her own body: "I have gotten a man with the help of the LORD" (Gen. 4:1) are the first words that Eve, the mother of all the living, utters in Scripture. Preserving this link between sexuality and the original Source of life is accordingly one special task that falls to the woman in marriage:

> This unique contact with the new human being developing within her gives rise to an attitude towards human beings—not only towards her own child, but every human being—which profoundly marks the woman's personality. It is commonly thought that *women* are more capable than men of paying attention *to another person*, and that motherhood develops this predisposition even more. (*MD*, 18)

Wojtyla then goes on to note that the father, unlike the mother, experiences his relationship with the child from the outside. In contrast to the woman, the man does not feel the connection to new life within his own body: "The man—even with all his sharing in parenthood—always remains 'outside' the process of pregnancy and the baby's birth; in many ways he has to *learn* his own '*fatherhood' from the mother*" (*MD*, 18). The father's role is to transform his distance from the child into an expression, not of cold indifference, but of the warmth of love. The father achieves this task, however, precisely by giving the child space to grow. If the father truly loves the child, this space is never empty, but is full of his liberating gift that fosters the child's own maturation in freedom.

Van Gogh captures the complementarity of the father and mother in a famous painting of a child taking his first steps.[5] On one side of the canvas, the mother supports the child in her arms, while on the other side the father waits with outstretched hands to receive him. Van Gogh's masterpiece reinforces John Paul II's point: Every child is meant to grow up in the double embrace of a mother, whose love literally surrounds and sustains him, and of a father, who awaits him from a distance that does not signify uninvolvement but the loving gift of an opportunity to grow and mature.

The fruitfulness of natural marriage does not end with the birth of the child, but spills over into the task of education. Both child-bearing and child rearing are ways in which natural marriage participates in the Creator's generous work of giving and sustaining life. The sacrament of marriage reinforces this participation within the fruitful love by which Christ gives birth to the Church. Not only do parents cooperate with God in giving and fostering human life; they also receive a new gift that crowns the first: They are entrusted with the transmission of the divine life that begins on earth and fully flowers in heaven. Christian parents are called to make the education of their children bear the fruit of life eternal. John Paul writes:

> As for marriage, one can deduce that—instituted in the context of the sacrament of creation in its totality, or in the state of original innocence—it was to serve not only to extend the work of creation, or procreation, but also to spread the same sacrament of creation to further generations of human beings, that is, to spread the supernatural fruits of man's eternal election by the Father in the eternal Son, the fruits man was endowed with by God in the very act of creation. (*TOB*, 506)

THE PROBLEM OF CONTRACEPTION

Conjugal love is by its very nature open to procreation. The sexual act that seals marital union is by definition also the gesture by which spouses signal their joint availability to receive the gift of new life (should it be given). John Paul II drew a lot of criticism for his uncompromising reaffirmation of this intrinsic connection between sexual union and openness to children. John Paul, a seasoned and intelligent pastor who was acquainted with every facet of marriage, knew perfectly well that sometimes spouses are unable to welcome a new child into the world. His rejection of contraception had nothing to do, then, with an inflexible demand that couples should try to have as many children as possible. Rather, the pope was warning us against the danger to our humanity posed by the apparently obvious "way out" that contraception seems to offer to couples who are unable to welcome a new family member. But what, exactly, did John Paul think was wrong with contraception? Since we use other technologies to modify our environment in the service of improving the quality of our lives, why *shouldn't* we apply contraceptive technology to our bodies to avoid the unwanted consequences of the conjugal act?

We begin our answer to this question by stressing that the body has a threefold meaning: There is the filial meaning of the body, inasmuch as the body expresses man's relationship with the Creator; and the body also is at once nuptial (ordered to union between the spouses) and procreative (open to the gift of a new life). These three dimensions are intimately connected in the one dynamism of love. In fact, man and woman can truly love each other only if they go beyond their own individuality in mutual self-giving (nuptial meaning). Such a gift is possible only if the partners receive their relationship from the Source of love (the filial meaning). Finally, rooted in the Source, as in the fertile soil from which their love springs, the union of the spouses bears new fruit (the procreative meaning). The inextricable interrelation of these meanings is especially obvious in the conjugal act, since the very embrace that crowns the union between the spouses is the act by which they betoken their shared readiness to welcome new life into the world. This is why the Church insists on the inseparability of what it calls the "unitive" and "procreative" dimensions of the conjugal act.

The child is the model embodiment of everything we mean by the "fruitfulness" of conjugal love, for the child is *the* token par excellence of God's presence in spousal union (as Gen. 4:1 tells us, Eve first recognizes the presence of God in human love when she conceives a child). Nevertheless, the fruitfulness of the conjugal union is not limited to the birth of a child. Every time the spouses grow beyond themselves and share the richness of their love with others, their union is fruitful in a broad sense. The same truth applies to the conjugal act, which is fruitful in this larger way whenever it promotes growth in love. It should be clear what we are driving at: Not every instance of the conjugal act has to result in a child in order to be fruitful in a way that is pleasing to God. Nevertheless, what every instance of the conjugal act *does* have to do in order to be fruitful is to respect the true nature of the conjugal act. Let's briefly look at how contraception obscures the truth of human love and so casts a shadow on the intimacy of spousal communion.

Everyone grants that contraceptives "deactivate" the procreative meaning of the conjugal union. But, someone might argue, don't couples who use contraceptives at least still hold on to the unitive meaning of sexuality? The answer is that they don't. This is because the unitive and procreative meanings of sexuality, far from being in conflict, are actually inseparably interconnected facets of the one dynamism of spousal love. Consequently, rendering either one of these "inoperative" is tantamount to weakening the whole movement of love. So how does suppression of the procreative dimension of human love rob the self-giving inherent in the conjugal act of its totality? How does contraception damage love in all its dimensions?

By effacing the procreative meaning of the body, contraception renders impossible the total gift of self to another (which is the essence of the unitive meaning of spousal love). Why does contraception have this effect? The answer is that it is a refusal to share the capacity of making the beloved fruitful. It is thanks to the man that the woman can become a mother, just as it is thanks to the woman that the man can become a father. As Pope Benedict says,

> The possibility of procreating a new human life is included in a married couple's integral gift of themselves. Since, in fact, every form of love endeavors to spread the fullness on which it lives, conjugal love has its own special way of communicating itself: the generation of children. Thus it not only resembles but also shares in the love of God who wants to communicate himself by calling the human person to life.[6]

By engaging in a contraceptive act, however, spouses attempt to get around this reality, for they withhold from each other the capacity to activate parental fruitfulness. Contraception, in a word, is a refusal to give and receive fruitfulness; it is a refusal, therefore, of the totality of the gift, and therefore the sexual act that includes contraception cannot fully express conjugal love. The point is not that every conjugal act must result in a child, but that any conjugal act that, like that involving contraception, refuses to express an *openness* to new life, impairs the spouses' capacity to express true love.

Since openness to fruitfulness is not just a consequence of conjugal love but an integral part of it, all the dimensions of the spouses' love are affected if this openness is impeded. First of all, the suppression of the procreative meaning of sex effaces the filial meaning of the body and thus damages its connection with the Source. This is because the language of the body isn't the spouses' creation, but echoes the voice of the Giver calling them to love. The spouses' acceptance of the language of the body, then, roots them in the Creator's love (and this rooting is a sine qua non for genuine marital communion). Conversely, when spouses suppress the procreative meaning of the body through contraception, they sever, or at least attenuate, their relationship with the Source. In other words, by deactivating the fruitfulness of sexual union, contraception excludes God's presence from conjugal love, thus cutting this love off from its deepest roots.

The damage contraception inflicts on the spouses' relationship with God has a double consequence in turn. The first thing contraception impairs is the spouses' ability to perceive each other's absolute dignity as the *imago Dei*. Moreover, since self-giving is based on a previous acceptance of oneself from the hands of the Creator, couples who use contraceptives also become less fully able to give themselves to each other. Either way, contraception, by clouding love's reference to the Creator, turns that love selfishly in on itself. By a kind of chain reaction, this refusal to be open to procreation then inclines the spouses to surrender to the urge for sexual satisfaction, which increasingly subjects them to a logic of necessity that displaces the logic of gift.

We'd like to stress the word "logic," which we have chosen to highlight a crucial distinction between the *nature* of the contraceptive act and the *motives* of couples who use contraceptives. It should be obvious that our concern is not only with why couples choose contraception, but also with how the use of contraception distorts the grammar of the body's language—often without couples being fully aware of this distortion.

NATURAL FAMILY PLANNING

We've already noted that the Catholic Church is quite aware that married couples may have serious reasons for deferring pregnancy in certain circumstances. The Church's response to this problem is not contraception but Natural Family Planning (NFP). This isn't to say, of course, that NFP is merely an alternative technique for achieving the same end as contraception, as if NFP were just a "natural" way of doing the same thing "artificial" methods of birth control are designed to achieve. Natural Family Planning is actually completely different from contraception. In fact, we call NFP "natural" precisely to highlight the fact that, unlike contraception, NFP respects the *nature* of human love, that is, the truth of spousal communion.

To begin with, lovers undermine each other's dignity as persons unless they cherish the truth of love. Second, the truth of love is revealed in love's natural aspiration to make a total gift of self. Third, it's only when lovers receive their love as a gift from God that they're capable of this total self-giving. Fourth and finally, to receive human love as God's gift is to respect the language of the body, in which God, the Author of this language, expresses himself and speaks his generous love.

As we've already noted, the Church has no problem acknowledging that couples sometimes have serious reasons for being unable to welcome more children into their family. The Church readily grants that such new situations may positively require some kind of change in how couples express their conjugal love. The point is simply that this change can't reflect the intimacy of spousal communion unless it respects the truth about love. Unfortunately, respecting the truth about love is precisely what contraception fails to do: By suppressing the procreative meaning of sexuality the spouses refuse to listen to the language of the body, given by the Creator himself. As a consequence, contraception diminishes and distorts the totality of self-giving, as we have considered in our last paragraph.

Natural Family Planning, by contrast, changes the expression of love (the spouses abstain from sex during the woman's fertile period), but not its essential truth: that the conjugal act is a total gift of self to the other person. For, rather than engineering sterility, spouses who use NFP respect the natural cycle of fertility. They do not suppress the procreative meaning of sexuality, but accept its presence, adapting themselves to the alternating periods of dormancy and fertility. By changing their sexual behavior, by adjusting the expression of their love to the natural rhythms built into the body's procreative meaning, spouses using NFP respect the truth that the bestowal of parenthood is an essential part of the total gift of self between the spouses. By the same token, NFP enables spouses to express due reverence for the Author of the body's language. Natural Family Planning keeps the spouses in connection with the Source of love, and this connection makes every act of love between the spouses fruitful (in the broad sense). As Pope Benedict XVI writes:

The methods of observation which enable the couple to determine the periods of fertility permit them to administer what the Creator has wisely inscribed in human nature without interfering with the integral significance of sexual giving. In this way spouses, respecting the full truth of their love, will be able to modulate its expression in conformity with these rhythms without taking anything from the totality of the gift of self that union in the flesh expresses. Obviously, this requires maturity in love which is not instantly acquired but involves dialogue and reciprocal listening, as well as a special mastery of the sexual impulse in a journey of growth in virtue.[7]

Natural Family Planning, then, is not a mere technique; it includes a whole education in sensitivity to the truth of love, an education that requires the involvement of the whole person. The practice of NFP transforms the spouses and their love, helping them to mature in mutual respect and to grow in appreciation for their vocation. If we take seriously what we have said so far, then we have to admit that "sex education" is a much more difficult, but also a much richer, affair than imparting familiarity with the mechanics of the sex act. The true education of sexuality is not about mastering a set of techniques, but about integrating all the dimensions of the person in accord with the truth of love. Real sex education fosters purity and piety, which in turn promote respect for the person and reverence for the sacredness of his or her body as God's temple. The gift of piety, writes John Paul II,

sustains and develops in the spouses a singular sensibility for all that in their vocation and shared life carries the sign of the mystery of creation and redemption: for all that is a created reflection of God's wisdom and love. For this reason, this gift seems to initiate man and woman particularly deeply into reverence for the two inseparable meanings [unitive and procreative] of the conjugal act. (*TOB*, 654)

It should be clear by now why John Paul II insisted on what he called the "moral" and the "anthropological" difference between contraception and NFP.[8] Let's start with the anthropological difference first, a difference in the ways in which the two methods understand the *meaning* of sexuality.

In NFP, as we have seen, sexuality is perceived as an occasion for total mutual self-giving. By practicing NFP, spouses adapt their sexual behavior to the rhythms of fecundity, in order to safeguard the totality of the gift, which they recognize as the core meaning of human sexuality. By contrast, contraception fosters the mentality that sexual intimacy is not an occasion for total gift of self, but a necessity to which man and woman are subjected. Couples who use contraceptives refuse to change their behavior. They insist on enjoying sex at the price of withholding the total gift of themselves. Again, the issue is not only the *motives* with which couples *enter into* contraception, but also the *deformation* of the heart with which they *come out* of it over time.

The anthropological difference between NFP and contraception obviously entails a profound moral difference between the methods as well. In the case of contraception, the spouses fail to adapt their sexual behavior to the truth of love, because they experience their sexuality as a necessity that compels them with an irresistible urge. With NFP the couple is able to change the sexual expression of their love because the sexual desire does not dominate them, since it has been integrated in the true love to the other person. In this way the spouses keep sexual desire from occupying the entire space of their relationship, and are thus liberated for the maturity that flourishes within the communion of persons. In a word, NFP is a response to the call to total gift of self, an education in chastity that enables couples to shape their relationship in accord with the truth of love in whatever situation of life they find themselves in.

CONJUGAL CHARITY AND THE CALL
TO HOLINESS

Marriage, sealed in faithfulness and fruitfulness, is a path to God. As such, it is by definition also a road to holiness, for holiness consists precisely in communion with the One who alone is holy. Holiness, in fact, is likeness to God, and this likeness grows as we journey to the fullness of the call to love as children, spouses, and parents.

If this is correct, then married couples don't have to look for the path to holiness outside their relationship. As John Paul II never tired of insisting, the spouses' mutual love *is* their path to God. The total gift marriage requires of them *is* their specific way of living out the Gospel and of becoming sharers in the divine nature. In fact, when they love each other "out of reverence for Christ," spouses don't just give themselves; they give to each other the Holy Spirit, the love of the Son and Bridegroom, who unites man and woman to one another and to God.

In her novel *Kristin Lavransdatter*, the Nobel Prize–winning Norwegian author Sigrid Undset captures this "sacramental" character of human love in a powerful image, which illustrates how God leads couples to holiness through their conjugal communion. Before her death, Undset's protagonist Kristin removes her wedding ring, which symbolizes her difficult love for her husband, Erlend, and recalls all the troubles of her life as a wife and a mother of seven children. As Kristin awaits the priest who will bring her the last oil and viaticum, she muses on the mark the ring has left on her finger:

> The last clear thought that took shape in her mind was that she was going to die before the mark had time to fade, and it made her happy. It seemed to her a mystery that she could not comprehend, but she was certain that God had held her firmly in a pact which had been made for her . . . from a love that had been poured over her—and . . . that love had stayed inside her, had worked on her like sun on the earth . . . under the glittering gold ring a mark had been secretly impressed upon her, showing that she was His servant, owned by the Lord and King who would now come, borne on the consecrated hand of the priest, to give her release and salvation.[9]

We began this chapter with the image of wedding rings, which signify the royal seal of God's presence and action that the marriage bond engraves in the life of the spouses. The mark impressed in the flesh by the wedding band is a complementary image. For this mark symbolizes the help that both spouses have been for each other on their shared journey toward the house of the Father. By the same token, the image of the ring-shaped mark in the flesh serves as a fitting transition to our next chapter, in which we will study the resurrection of that very flesh and the consequences this resurrection has for the theology of the body.

CHAPTER 9

WITNESSING TO THE FULLNESS OF LOVE: CHRISTIAN VIRGINITY AND THE DESTINY OF THE BODY

JOHN PAUL II'S *THEOLOGY OF THE BODY* STARTS WITH A retrieval of the original experiences that lie at the foundation of human existence. But the beginning is only half the story; it reveals a good deal of the Creator's original plan, but it does not disclose the whole of it. In order to understand the full picture, we need more than the beginning. We also need to look at the end, in which our journey reaches its final destination.

Is it possible to glimpse something of the end, just as we have glimpsed something of the beginning? At first sight, the answer seems to be no, for the end appears to be more elusive than the beginning. After all, the beginning lies behind and beneath us, like the solid foundations of a house or the tenacious roots of a vigorous tree. By contrast, the end—our final destiny—can seem ethereal and intangible by comparison; it can appear as insubstantial as the fleeting images of summer fruit that pass before the mind's eye as we stare at winter's barren branches. On reflection, though, we have to agree with John Paul II that the end, no less than the beginning, is somehow present in our experience (*TOB*, 397). As the pope writes apropos of Michaelangelo's *Last Judgment*, the end isn't completely hidden but already sheds its light on man's journey of love:

> In the very center of the Sistine Chapel, the artist
> depicts this invisible End
> in the visible drama of the Judgment—
> This invisible End has become visible as the
> height of transparency. (*RT*, 22)

John Paul II was not naive. He knew better than most of us that the "invisible End" is not just the "height of transparency"; it is also an unknown future that casts a shadow of fear over us as we journey inevitably toward death:

> And so the generations pass—
> naked they come into the world and naked they return
> to the earth from which they were formed.
> "From dust you came, and to dust you shall return":
> What had shape is now shapeless.
> What was alive is now dead.
> What was beautiful is now the ugliness of decay. (*RT*, 22)

John Paul II was anything but ingenuous, then, about the decay and ugliness that await us. At the same time, he insisted that this fate is not the whole truth about man's end. After the rather dark lines we just cited, John Paul introduces a note of hope: "And yet I do not altogether die, / what is indestructible in me remains!" (*RT*, 22).

When we ponder our destiny, we are apt to be visited by anxious questions: What will remain of all the struggles to reach the perfection of love that we have described in this book? What will become of the lovers' joy in each other? Will anything be left of the mother's exultation over the gift of a child? Do the happiness we have enjoyed and the suffering we have endured possess any ultimate significance? John Paul II's ringing proclamation of "what is indestructible in" man directs our gaze to the answer to these questions and gives us hope that the arduous journey of love is worthwhile. As we will see, this answer is nothing less than the resurrection of the body.

THE BODY REVEALS LIFE AND DEATH

In the book of Genesis, God warns man that as soon as he eats from the tree of the knowledge of good and evil, *he will die* (Gen. 2:17). Man's awareness of the possibility of death accompanies him from the very beginning. This awareness, which sets him apart from the animals, is in fact woven by the fragility of the body into the experience of original solitude itself. In our everyday experience, it is the body—through disease and aging—that reminds us that we are mortal and that we are anything but the source of our own life. Man, the Bible reminds us, is "flesh, a wind that passes and comes not again" (Ps. 78:39).

Ironically, the experience of love often seems to throw the fragility of the flesh into even sharper relief. After all, love doubles our fear, for the lover is anxious not only for his own well-being, but for the welfare of his beloved as well. This twofold anxiety prompts the question the Jeweler addresses to Teresa and Andrew in *The Jeweler's Shop*:

How can it be done, Teresa,
for you to stay in Andrew forever?

How can it be done, Andrew,
for you to stay in Teresa forever
since man will not endure in man
and man will not suffice? (*JS*, 41)

The body, then, reveals that we are doomed to die. There is no getting around the unyielding fact of death. Nevertheless, the inevitability of our demise is not the only thing that the body teaches us. As
we've seen, the body is also the key to experiencing life as openness
and relationship beyond the limits of mere self-sufficiency. Admittedly, our bodily condition exposes us to the world, yet this exposure
is not just fragility. It is also strength. Our openness to the world is
the doorway to true life, the pathway to that life in abundance we
come to enjoy through communion with others.

The insight that life is communion underlies the Old Testament's
conception of man. For the ancient Hebrews, being alive meant participating in a concrete relationship with the world, with others, and
with God. Since they saw the body as the basis of this relationship,
the Jews struggled at first with the idea of life after death. Their rea-
soning is not hard to follow: If life is relationship, and relationship
is bodily, wouldn't bodily death put an end to all relationship and
so rule out any full-blooded sense of the afterlife? Not surprisingly,
the Old Testament initially pictured the underworld, or Sheol as the
Hebrews called it, as a domain of shades, hovering on the margins
of existence, who would never again see the light or share in Israel's
praise of God.

At this point, we need to recall that the body's openness to others
and to the world is ultimately an openness to God. Man's original
solitude finds no final resting place in the other creatures around
him. This is because man, unlike the animals, is a partner of the Ab-

solute, who is the true beginning and end of human existence. Now, if man's life is relationship, and relationship is ultimately with God, the Source of life, then man must somehow continue in existence even beyond the apparently final word of death. It must somehow be the case that, "though my flesh and my heart fail, God is the strength of my heart and my portion for ever" (Ps. 73:26). The body must in some way witness to an indestructible relationship with God that heralds the ultimate triumph of life over death. Once again, the body not only reminds us that we are mortal; it also teaches us to hope for life in abundance.

By pondering the relation to God that gives man life, the Old Testament gradually discovered the true nature of our call to immortality. In response to the Sadducees' sneering attempt to discredit this biblical hope, Jesus reaffirms the promise of the resurrection: "And as for the resurrection of the dead, have you not read what was said to you by God, 'I am the God of Abraham, and the God of Isaac, and the God of Jacob'? He is not God of the dead, but of the living" (Matt. 22:31–32). Behind Jesus's rebuke is a gripping piece of logic: First, God's choice to enter into a covenant with the Patriarchs means that he has tied his own name—and so his very identity—to these men. Moreover, God is the living God of Israel and is himself the source of life. Consequently, Abraham, Isaac, and Jacob, though dead in an earthly sense, must still have a place within the covenant the living God once made with them. Since the Creator has established a covenant with them, they must somehow remain in relationship with the Creator and thus continue to receive life from his divine hand. As John Paul II puts it in *Roman Triptych*, man's end is to return to the Source of life from which he came: "The End is as invisible as the Beginning. The universe came forth from the Word, and returns to the Word" (*RT*, 22).

"LOVE IS STRONG AS DEATH" (SONG 8:6)

The Bible's understanding of life as relationship with God is reflected in its approach to love between man and woman. Because the original unity of Adam and Eve reveals God as the Giver and Source of love, their love is endowed with a certain immortality. God's presence emboldens love to fight back against the forces of decay and to prove that it is "strong as death" (Song 8:6). As Karol Wojtyla once wrote, "love does not flow from death, it runs beyond" (*Collected Poems*, 131). Once again, the language of the body speaks paradoxically in one breath of man's fragility and of his power to triumph over death: "The body conceals within itself the prospect of death, to which love does not want to submit. In fact . . . love is 'a flame of the Lord' that 'the great waters cannot quench . . . / neither can the rivers drown it' (Song 8:6–7)" (*TOB*, 586).

The book of Tobit vividly depicts love's dramatic struggle with death. The story's protagonist, Tobias, knowingly marries a woman—Sarah—whose previous seven bridegrooms have been killed on their wedding night by the demon Asmodeus. Knowing that their love is threatened by the forces of destruction and death, Tobias and Sarah invoke God's protection in the confidence that, just as he once blessed marriage in Eden, he will faithfully fulfill this original promise in their lives as well:

> When the door was shut and the two were alone, Tobias got up from the bed and said, "Sister, get up, and let us pray that the Lord may have mercy upon us." And Tobias began to pray, "Blessed art thou, O God of our fathers, and blessed be thy holy and glorious name for ever. Let the heavens and all thy creatures

bless thee. Thou madest Adam and gavest him Eve his wife as a helper and support. From them the race of mankind has sprung. Thou didst say, 'It is not good that the man should be alone; let us make a helper for him like himself.' And now, O Lord, I am not taking this sister of mine because of lust, but with sincerity. Grant that I may find mercy and may grow old together with her." And she said with him, "Amen." (Tob. 8:4–8)

The story of Tobias and Sarah underscores that the original blessing God bestows on human love is more powerful than the dark forces that threaten to overwhelm it. As we said just now, God's presence empowers human love with a vigor that is stronger than death and destruction. This strength sheds light in turn on the enigmatic words of John Paul II that we cited at the beginning of the chapter: "What is indestructible in me remains" (RT, 22). The pope is telling us that human love reveals "what is indestructible in man," and that this indestructible force is man's relationship with the Source of life. Human love is a participation in God's eternity. Love's anchoring in God's eternal life undergirds the truth of French philosopher Gabriel Marcel's remark that "to love a being is to say: Thou, Thou shall not die."[1]

But let's not be too hasty. Even if God's blessing and promise embolden love to challenge death, doesn't death always win the contest in the end? Doesn't it always finally separate us from our loved ones? The same body that rejoices the heart with a glimpse of fulfillment also mercilessly brings home to us the inevitability of disease and decay. Man's strength is at once his weakness, and the body appears too fragile to capture the immortality it seems to promise. Can we seriously hope for any way out of this impasse?

We shouldn't be surprised if human love is unable to solve the problem that it itself poses. This inability is actually what the whole pattern of man's existence should lead us to expect. At every crucial turn on the journey of love, in fact, we've seen that further growth depends on the intervention of, or the encounter with, outside assistance. If man's existence is relationship, it's fitting that the solution to the riddle it poses should lie in expectation and hope. The only question is what we should place this hope in.

THE FULFILLMENT OF SONSHIP

For a Christian, the answer is clear: The Resurrection of Jesus Christ from the dead is the source of our hope. The Fathers of the Church never tired of repeating that the Good News of the Christian Gospel isn't that the soul somehow survives death. Plato and Aristotle had already guessed that. No, the Good News the Fathers celebrated was the resurrection of the body. They never got over their amazement at the core Christian message that Jesus rose from the dead, and that our fragile and humble bodies will one day rise into incorruptible glory with him. The Gospel rang out as glad tidings in the gloom of late antiquity, not simply because it promised the survival of the soul, but mainly because Jesus's Resurrection opened to human love a new and living way beyond the fear of death.

Consider for a moment Jesus's earthly life, which brings the ideal of the Old Testament to its fulfillment. God's plan to give man a share in his own life reaches its—for us—unexpected culmination in the sending of his only Son. The God *of Abraham, Isaac, and Jacob* now fully unveils his identity as the "God and Father *of our Lord Jesus Christ*" (2 Cor. 1:3). God's decision to tie his name to the Patriarchs reaches its (surprising) apex in the mission of the Son, who fully reveals the divine name and entwines it forever with man's destiny.

The Son of God has existed from all eternity, and his being consists in pure filial relationship with the Father. The Incarnation doesn't change this filial identity. Instead Christ's flesh expresses his eternal Sonship within the limits of concrete human existence. We perceive the fittingness of this arrangement when we recall that the human body itself has a filial meaning, insofar as it is an openness to God. Christ's body takes this native openness and transforms it into an expression of filial love that is saturated by his communion with the Father. Christ's body is sheer relation to the Father, and it is saturated by the very love that unites the Father and the Son.

We've seen that life is relationship with God. We can now add that life is *filial* relationship with him. This insight reveals new meaning in Jesus's progressive fulfillment of Sonship, which we studied in Part II of the book. Christ, we recall, communicates the fullness of filiation in our flesh. But Sonship, we now see, *is* the very essence of life. Therefore, Christ's gift of filiation is also the gift of eternal life to the human race.

Paradoxically, Christ's life-giving revelation of Sonship culminated on the Cross. It was on the Cross that the Spirit's hands molded the clay of Jesus's bodily suffering and death into the supreme masterpiece of incarnate filial love. Christ's total obedience to the Father in the Spirit sowed the seed of immortality in his body during his earthly life, and Christ's death was the beginning of his victory over death.

The fact that the Cross is already a triumph over death does not make the Resurrection superfluous. On the contrary, the Resurrection brings to light the fruit of Christ's death and so crowns his earthly mission, which culminated on Calvary. By raising Jesus from the dead, the Father irrevocably seals Jesus's body as a life-giving expression of Christ's eternal Sonship. In the Acts of the Apostles, Peter uses Psalm 2 to highlight the new birth the eternal Son experiences in his risen flesh for our sakes: "And we bring you the good news that what God promised to the fathers, this he has fulfilled to us their children by raising Jesus; as also it is written in the second psalm, 'Thou art my Son, today I have begotten thee' " (Acts 13:32–33).

The Resurrection crowns the progressive "filialization" of Christ's flesh that began with his conception. By the same token, the Resurrection frees Christ's flesh, which opens up to include the human race in the same life-giving filial love that permeates him. As the second-century theologian Tertullian writes apropos of the final resurrection of the blessed: "he called them 'the children of the resurrection,' for by the resurrection, in a sort of way, they have to be born."[2] But what happens when Christ raises up our bodies? What does it mean to be a "child of the resurrection"?

According to Saint Paul, the final resurrection will give us what he calls a "spiritual" body (see 1 Cor. 15:44). Typically, we tend to define the spirit as the opposite of the body, which we generally identify with the material part of man. Obviously, as long as we continue to pit the spirit against the body, their combination in the phrase "spiritual body" sounds like a contradiction in terms. The only way to resolve the contradiction would be to interpret the "spiritual body" as a dematerialized, ethereal ghost. Happily, Paul is inviting us to contemplate a much more appealing picture of our future. In order to see this picture we need to redefine the word "spiritual" in relation to the *Holy Spirit*. For once we recall that the Spirit is the bond of love between the Father and the Son, and that the body is openness to God's love, the contradiction disappears. Far from being in conflict, spirit and body are in perfect accord, because the Spirit is the divine love the body was originally created to contain and express. By the same happy logic, the coming of the Holy Spirit in the Resurrection does not destroy the body but brings it to perfection and fulfills its meaning.[3] It's this fulfillment that will occupy our attention in what follows.

CHRIST AND THE FULFILLMENT OF NUPTIALITY

We've focused so far on how the Resurrection crowns the total expression of Sonship in and through Christ's body. But Jesus is also the Bridegroom who crowns his love for the Father by loving his brothers and sisters. Christ's spousal love for humanity reaches its pinnacle in the Resurrection. Indeed, Jesus's risen flesh is itself the embodied fullness of his love for his fellow men. The Risen Lord himself assures us of this: "Go to my brethern and say to them . . . I am ascending to my father and your father, to my God and your God" (John 20:17). In revealing the Fatherhood of God, Jesus also establishes the brotherhood of God's children. John Paul writes:

> We should think of the reality of the "other world" in the categories of the rediscovery of a new, perfect subjectivity of each person and at the same time of the *rediscovery* of a new, *perfect intersubjectivity of all*. In this way this reality means the true and definitive fulfillment of human subjectivity and, on this basis, the definitive fulfillment of the "spousal" meaning of the body. (*TOB*, 396)

Just as Christ's risen body is a pure expression of his Sonship, it is total openness to others. Being totally *filial*, it is also totally *nuptial* as well. Having received everything from the Father, Christ is able to give everything to the Church, his Bride. Christ's Resurrection so completely fulfills the nuptial meaning of the body that Christ's relationship with his Bride, the Church, is the model we have to look to if we want to understand the true depth of love between man and woman. The love between Christ and his Church is the archetype of natural marriage, and natural marriage was created to become a sacramental image of the bond between Christ and his Church.

The first couple—like all couples after them—are called to live their spousal self-gift as a total commitment to each other. The exclusivity of this commitment is necessary for each partner to honor the other's uniqueness as a reflection of the Absolute. Christ's nuptial communion with his Church fulfills this experience of Adam and Eve yet is not simply a "rerun" that reproduces their relationship in literal detail. For, while Jesus's nuptial self-giving is also an intimate embrace of each one of us in our individual uniqueness and originality, Christ's ability to give himself totally to others doesn't require an exclusive commitment to each one of us of the sort involved in earthly marriage. Christ can give himself completely to each individual while simultaneously giving himself up "for many" others at the same time (see Mark 14:24). The supreme expression of this miracle of intimacy without exclusivity is the Eucharist. The Eucharist contains, after all, the body Christ gave up at once "for me," as a unique and unrepeatable person (see Gal. 2:20), and "for all" (see 1 Tim. 2:6), who therefore become my brothers and sisters by sharing in the same risen flesh of Christ that I share in. Through the Eucharist, the Risen Christ communicates his life to all Christians, as one burning candle spreads its flame to others during the Easter Vigil, as is described in a homily from the Church Fathers:

> Just as the body of the Lord was glorified on the mountain when it was transfigured in the glory of God and in infinite light, so the bodies of the saints will be glorified and shine like lightning... "The glory which thou hast given me I have given to them" [John 17:22]. As countless candles are lighted from a single flame, so the bodies of all Christ's members will be what Christ is... Our human nature is transformed into the fullness of God; it becomes wholly fire and light.[4]

"NEITHER MARRY NOR ARE GIVEN IN MARRIAGE" (LUKE 20:35)

Catholics believe that the saints in heaven enjoy a share in Christ's ability to give himself fully to each individual without exclusivity. A corollary of this belief is that the exclusivity of the marriage bond drops away in the next life, as Jesus himself teaches in the Gospel: "those who are deemed worthy to attain to that age and to the resurrection from the dead," he says, "neither marry nor are given in marriage" (Luke 20:35). How are we to understand this teaching? What happens to the relationship between spouses in heaven? Is Christ saying that the blessed are so totally absorbed by the presence of God that their fellow creatures—including their earthly spouses—simply fade into the background of their God-soaked consciousness?

The first point we need to stress is that the resurrection will not abolish man's bodily nature but will transform it. By the same logic, the risen life will not do away with our masculinity and femininity; it will transfigure them with the light of divine love. Human beings will not cease to be male and female, yet they will experience their sexuality in a qualitatively new way. John Paul writes:

> Human bodies, which are recovered and also renewed in the resurrection, will preserve their specific masculine or feminine character and... *the meaning of being male or female in the body* will be *constituted and understood differently* in the "other world" than it had been "from the beginning" and then in its whole earthly dimension... "The dimension of masculinity and femininity, that is, being male and female in the body—will be newly constituted in the resurrection of the body in that 'other world.' (*TOB*, 388)

What is the nature of the transformation of our sexual being that the pope places before the eyes of our hope in this text? There is a wonderful passage in the *Divine Comedy* that points us in the direction of an answer to this question. As he journeys through purgatory, Dante learns from Virgil, his guide, that in heaven there is no envy among the blessed: "For there, the more who say, 'This joy is ours,' / the more joy is possessed by every soul." This observation prompts the poet to ask:

> How can something good, if shared by more,
> make each one's portion richer in its worth
> than if the same thing were possessed by few?

In answer to Dante's question, Virgil compares God's love to a light reflected by a number of mirrors. The more polished each mirror is, the more light it reflects, not only for itself, but also for others:

And the more souls that burn in Heaven above,
as mirrors flashing light on one another,
the more there is for all of them to love.[5]

Virgil's point is clear: Intimate communion with God does not isolate us from one another but unites us in the closest possible way. If we apply the same logic to the relation between man and woman—which is what we want to focus on here—we can say that it's only when the two draw fully from the primordial Giver that they are empowered to give themselves fully to each other. Communion with God spills over into the relations between spouses, welding them into what the Apostles' Creed calls "the communion of saints."

The transformation of the spouses' relationship in God does not destroy their earthly love but transfigures it. It's easier to understand this point if we recall that conjugal love does not eliminate original solitude; rather original solitude remains at the core of (and is even enhanced by) original unity. The continuation of original solitude in the midst of nuptial communion builds what John Paul II calls a "virginal dimension" into the relation between the spouses. Spousal love can be virginal because the partners—and their relation—belong to God before they belong to each other. In fact, it's only because they belong first to God that they can even belong to each other at all. By the same token, the gift of unreserved belonging to God in heaven—which is the full flowering of the virginal dimension, already a fundamental element in spousal love—will not destroy this love, but will transfigure it with a new light. The heavenly experience of the body's virginal depth is not opposed to its spousal meaning but brings that meaning to its supreme fulfillment (*TOB*, 395).

Another way of expressing the virginal basis of spousal love is that Adam can love Eve as a wife only if he respects her as a daughter of

God (and vice versa). Similarly, in heaven the spouses share in the peace that the Song of Songs ascribes to the bridegroom, whose purity enables him to address his beloved bride as a "sister." In heaven, then, the spouses discover each other as brother and sister in a "common sense of belonging to the Creator as their common Father" (*TOB*, 566). As they draw ever closer to the Source of gift, the spouses grow more deeply into the peace of communion that unites them as children of the same Father:

> The words of the bridegroom addressed to the bride as "sister" as well as her words in the same relation are impregnated with a particular content. Love . . . pushes both to seek the common past as though they descended from the same family circle, as though from infancy they had been united by memories of the common hearth. In this way, they reciprocally feel as close as brother and sister who owe their existence to the same mother. A specific sense of common belonging follows from this . . . From here, consequently, arises the peace that the bride speaks of. It is the "peace of the body," which in appearance resembles sleep ("Do not rouse, do not stir up the beloved until she wants it"). It is above all the peace of the encounter in humanity as the image of God—and the encounter by means of a reciprocal and disinterested gift. (*TOB*, 566)

It is precisely because once in heaven man and woman draw directly from the Source of life that they no longer marry or are given in marriage.

This doesn't mean, however, that the resurrection robs matrimony of its importance. On the contrary, it fully reveals the true grandeur of the sacrament, which reached into Eternity even while the spouses still walked the earth. Like the mirrors of which Dante speaks, the closer they come to the Source of light, the more they both give light to others and perceive the beauty of others' light in turn.

What we've just said consolingly illumines the situation of spouses who live on as widows or widowers after the death of their husbands or wives. Death is not a final separation, or a last word that puts an end to their relation, for their love lives on transformed. God's love, which was always an essential part of their earthly love, is now expressed in a new way with the primacy it always had in the first place. The challenge the widowed face is to learn how to live with this new presence of the deceased partner, relating to his or her renewed existence in the sphere of the God of the Resurrection. The life of the widow or widower is thus a preparation for a new encounter in which his or her earthly love will be transformed, purified, and strengthened in the embrace of God who will be all in all.

Let's sum up what we've said so far about the positive transformation of marriage in heaven, a transformation that changes the expression of earthly love, even as it fulfills its deepest substance. Recall our definition of purity of heart as the capacity to see the presence of God in the union of love between man and woman. Applying this definition to the foregoing discussion, we can say that the Resurrection fulfills and transfigures earthly marriage precisely by bringing conjugal chastity to its perfection. The Resurrection is the supreme integration of all the dimensions of love described in chapter 2—so that every step the spouses take toward purity in their earthly life prepares their bodies for immortality and sows in them seeds of the Resurrection.

THE CALL TO VIRGINITY

Christ transforms human love: "Our Lord," writes Karol Wojtyla, "accomplishes so much through love, so much good. Love joins us with Him more than anything else because it transforms everything" (*OGB*, 210). Of course, this transformation isn't reserved only for the next life in heaven. Already here and now it is both a gift and a challenge for spouses, whom Christ calls to draw their common life from the fullness of his own love as Son and Bridegroom. Our task now is to round out the picture by showing how Christ establishes a new way of answering the call to love alongside marriage. It is time, then, to consider what the Church calls "the state of consecrated virginity."

It's interesting to note that the Old Testament does not value virginity but instead exalts marriage as the royal road to union with God. As the third-century Church Father Saint Methodius of Olympus says: "It was reserved for the Lord alone to be the first to exalt this doctrine [of virginity] . . . It was only fitting that He who was Archpriest, Archprophet, and Archangel, should also be called Archvirgin."[6]

There is just one apparent exception to the Old Testament's exaltation of marriage: the story of the prophet Jeremiah, who remains unmarried by the Lord's command. Nevertheless, Jeremiah's celibacy reflects an exceptional call to embody the desolation of Israel, who had strayed from the Lord and become a lifeless people whose streets no longer rang with the joyous song of the bride and the bridegroom. In a word, the story of Jeremiah is only an apparent exception that actually confirms the Old Testament rule, for the prophet experiences—and is meant to experience—his virginity simply as a lack of fulfillment. By contrast, Christ experienced virginity not as a lack but as an overflowing plenitude of love. Christ, the Son and the Bridegroom, reveals in his own flesh that virginity is the highest summit of the spousal meaning of the body itself:

> In the light of Christ's words . . . one can deduce that [a person's] *renunciation* [of marriage] *is at the same time a particular form of affirmation of the value* from which the unmarried person consistently abstains by following the evangelical counsel. [The realization of virginity] serves also . . . to confirm the spousal meaning of the human body in its masculinity and femininity. The renunciation of marriage for the kingdom of God at the same time highlights that meaning in all its inner truth and in all its personal beauty. (*TOB*, 441)

Ever the realist, John Paul II makes no secret of the "renunciation" demanded of consecrated virgins who must give up marriage if they wish to follow in Christ's footsteps. The pope knows, then, that celebrating the newness of Christian virginity doesn't require pretending that it is painless. John Paul means that consecrated virginity isn't new because it makes the renunciation of marriage painless, but because it transforms even that pain into a joyful affirmation of the "spousal meaning of the human body."

The pope bases this transforming power of consecrated virginity on the bedrock of the Resurrection. Christ's flesh, now totally permeated by the Spirit of love, communicates to the disciples the fullest experience of the body as a "place" of communion. This is why John Paul calls the virginal meaning of the body "eschatological," a word derived from the Greek for "end": *eschaton*. Virginity, the pope is saying, points to the end of history; it is a participation in, and a testimony to, the fullness of love that already streams from Christ's risen body and that will flood the physical universe when he returns at the end of time. Or, as Maximus Confessor puts it, "the Word comes to dwell in the saints by imprinting on them in advance, in a mystery, the form of his future advent, as an icon."[7] As we'll see in a moment, this eschatological horizon is the key to how virginity fulfills the threefold pattern of filiation, nuptiality, and paternity we looked at in the last chapter.

VIRGINITY: THE FULFILLMENT OF FILIATION, NUPTIALITY, AND PATERNITY

We saw in the last chapter that the threefold pattern of childhood, spousehood, and parenthood serves Christ as a language for expressing in the flesh the fullness of his love as both Son and Bridegroom. We can now add that virginity plays a central role in the "adaptation" of the threefold pattern of the body to the requirements of the Son's mission. First, Christ's embrace of the virginal meaning of the body begins with his exclusive dedication to the Father's will. Christ's flesh is virginal because it is filial. Far from denigrating the spousal meaning of the body, however, Christ's virginity—and this is the second point—affirms and fulfills it. As we saw earlier, it's not that Christ enters into an ordinary earthly marriage; it's that he fulfills ordinary earthly marriage by transforming it into a sacramental image of his spousal relation with the Church. The Son, in other words, is also the Bridegroom who generates, and unites himself to, the Church on the Cross. Third and finally, Christ's spousal union with his Bride is supremely fruitful; through baptism, Christ begets sons and daughters for the Father from the womb of the Church. The three-fold pattern inscribed in the body is thus complete: Christ's virginity, rooted in filial obedience, fulfills the body's nuptial meaning. In bringing nuptiality to completion, moreover, the virginal Christ also fully lives out the call to parental fruitfulness that is inscribed in it.

What, then, about Christians who are called to follow their Master in consecrated virginity? In the words of the early Church Father Saint Ignatius of Antioch, their task is to "honor the flesh of the Lord."[8] Consecrated virgins, then, receive the privilege of becoming configured to Christ's own body and so of sharing in the fulfillment of the threefold pattern of human love Christ achieves through his Cross and Resurrection. Let's briefly consider each aspect of this triple call.

In Christ, the Son: Fulfillment of Original Solitude

The core of virginity is a new filial relationship with the Father that Christ communicates to us through his Incarnation and his subsequent life in the flesh. In becoming man, remember, the Son confers on his flesh a new capacity to express the presence of God and so establishes a new measure for the human body. Christ lives out in his own body the filial relation that eternally unites him to the Father. The consecrated person, for his part, is called to participate in the Lord's revelation of Sonship in the flesh. Consecrated virginity, we could say, is the gift and task of manifesting the true face of original solitude, which is precisely the face of Sonship. The body of the con-

secrated person is meant to be a sign of the primacy of the Father's
love in the midst of the world.

In Christ, the Bridegroom: Fulfillment of Original Unity

Consecrated persons participate in Christ's fulfillment of the nuptial meaning of the body. In Christ and like him, the consecrated
are called to embody the self-giving of the Bridegroom, who loves all
men, not as an indifferentiated mass, but with an exquisite sensitivity to the uniqueness and particularity of each single person.

It bears stressing that this fulfillment of the filial and nuptial
meanings of the body is itself rooted in the actual flesh of consecrated
persons and that it touches their affectivity and passions. Saint Paul
reminds us of this crucially important point when he describes the
consecrated virgin's new way of living in the body in terms of "anxiety" (which, as we know, is part of the body's affective repertoire).
Just as the married man is anxious about how he may please his wife,
Paul writes in 1 Corinthians 7:32–34, the unmarried man is anxious "about the things of the Lord, how he may please the Lord."

According to Paul, then, the consecrated virgin is not free from
anxiety; he or she does not live in some spiritual paradise alien to the
sorrows and joys of this world of ours. Just the opposite: He or she is
anxious to please the Lord, shares Jesus's bodily anxiety for the salvation of the world, and partakes of the sufferings and joys that the Lord
underwent for all men. The virgin lives out spousal love for the Lord by
sharing in the anguish and hope of all men through the compassionate
heart of Christ. As Saint Paul says: "there is the daily pressure upon me
of my anxiety for all the churches" (2 Cor. 11:28). Of course, this anxi-

ety is rooted in God's peace, in the security that the Father's love will never fail: The Father "who did not spare his own Son but gave him up for us all, will he not also give us all things with him?" (Rom. 8:32).

Spiritual Fatherhood and Motherhood

Saint Paul's remarks about celibacy remind us of the easily forgotten truth that consecrated virginity is no purely ethereal affair but fulfills the nuptial meaning of the body. The Pauline emphasis on the full-bodied character of consecrated virginity naturally calls for the complementary insight that consecrated virginity is fruitful. As Saint Augustine said, virginity is not sterile but flowers in spiritual fatherhood and motherhood. In order to appreciate fully Augustine's point in the following quote, we need to remember that the adjective "spiritual" does not refer to some ghostly opposite of matter but to the transfiguration of the body in the Holy Spirit. The saint is talking about a vision he had right before his conversion: "There were large numbers of boys and girls, a multitude of all ages, young adults and grave widows and elderly virgins. In every one of them was Continence herself, in no sense barren but the fruitful mother of children, the joys born of you, Lord, her husband."⁹

The French poet Paul Claudel captures the fruitfulness of virginity in his play *The Tidings Brought to Mary*. The main character of the drama, Violaine, having contracted leprosy while caring for a man infected with the disease, lives in isolation from her family. She accepts this isolation as an expression of her faith in, and obedience to, God. Paradoxically, the only person who understands the secret of Violaine's holiness is the one who despises her the most: her sister Mara. Thus, when Mara's child dies, Mara asks Violaine to raise the dead infant to life. Violaine's embrace revives Mara's daughter, but it also transforms her: The child's eyes are now the same color as Violaine's. "Violaine!" Mara exclaims,

> What does this mean?
> Its eyes were black,
> And now they are blue like yours. (Silence.)
> Ah!
> And what is this drop of milk I see on its lips?[10]

Violaine, Claudel is telling us, is a spiritual mother; her sufferings were the labor pains by which she bore her dead niece to new life. Indeed, at the end of the play, Violaine's father interprets his daughter's fruitful sacrifice in light of Mary's yes at the Annunciation: "Be it done to me according to thy word." In conclusion, we'll look at how Mary, the Mother of Jesus, embodies the fruitfulness of virginity.

MARY, MOTHER OF VIRGINS

Mary, the Mother of Jesus, is the living, breathing model of virginity. Mary's virginal motherhood takes up and transforms the same three meanings of the body that Christ lives out as Son and fruitful Bridegroom.

Filiation

We've already seen that God is at work every time a mother conceives new life in her womb. But God was never more actively involved in the process of generating new human life than when Mary conceived Christ—"the son of a virgin, who himself was a virgin" (*TOB*, 442)—without a human father. Mary's virginal motherhood, which manifests the Father as the absolute origin and source of all life, shares uniquely in the fulfillment of the filial meaning of the body achieved by her Son. Indeed, Mary lives totally for the work and person of Jesus and her only anxiety is to listen to, and serve, his word.

Nuptiality

By the same logic, Mary's participation in the fulfillment of filiation spills over into a participation in the fulfillment of nuptiality. At the foot of the Cross, Mary shares in the sufferings of Christ on our behalf and thus becomes an icon of the Church, the fruitful Bride of the Lamb.

Parenthood

Finally, Mary's motherhood, whether in Nazareth or on Calvary, is intimately bound up with Christ's fulfillment of the parental meaning of the body. Mary is the supreme embodiment of motherhood's openness to the gift of God. Mary is blessed among all women, because, as Dante puts it, "in [her] womb was the flame of love reborn."[11]

THE REALISM of Mary's involvement in Jesus's birth in Bethlehem and in his rebirth and formation in every Christian's life reminds us once again that the consecrated virgin's fruitfulness is not disembodied. Mary's virginal motherhood demonstrates precisely the opposite. Just as her motherhood marks the beginning of the new creation, consecrated virginity is the voice of "the whole creation . . . groaning in travail together until now," or, to vary the metaphor, the face of man's expectant longing for "the redemption of our bodies" (see Rom. 8:22–23). Far from being purely "spiritual" in the conventional sense of "ethereal" or "ghostly," Marian virginity literally embodies the answer to God's call to shape the material world into an expression of his love.

Like Mary, the consecrated person follows in Jesus's footsteps along the path of the child, the spouse, and the parent. Like Mary, he or she lives out a "preview" of the fulfillment of the threefold familial pattern in heaven. Of course, all Christians are called to anticipate this heavenly consummation of filiation, nuptiality, and parenthood in one way or another. Nothing we've said about virginity in this chapter implies the slightest exclusion of married couples from Christian holiness. On the contrary, marriage and consecrated virginity are intimately related, and even complementary. The mutual dedication of the spouses serves consecrated men and women as a reminder that virginity is no escape from the concrete visibility of Christian life in the body. For its part, consecrated life reminds married couples of the goal of their love in God and keeps ever before their eyes the urgency of their vocation to love one another in the great mystery of Christ's love.

What we have said in this chapter also illuminates the journey of singles who, through no fault of their own, haven't found a place in one of these two states of life. Like every man and woman, singles participate in the common vocation to love and embody the triple pattern of child, spouse, and parent. They are called to find concrete ways to offer their lives—in their work in society and in their service to those in need—as a fruitful gift to others in such a way as to lead them to God. Pope John Paul II wrote: "No one is without a family in this world: the Church is a home and family for everyone." (*Familiaris Consortio*, 85). The Church is the great family in which everyone has a place at the table; it is "a sign and instrument both of a very closely knit union with God and of the unity of the whole human race" (*LG*, 1). The family anticipates the pattern of the Church's unity, and this anticipation gives rise to a mission whose nature and dynamism will occupy us in the final chapter of this book.

CHAPTER 10

THE FAMILY AND THE CIVILIZATION OF LOVE

THE LIFE OF THE FAMILY WAS THE GREAT THEME WHOSE harmonies we sounded in the preceding chapters of this book. This focus on the pattern of family life in no way implies, however, that the family's significance stops at its own borders. The whole tenor of our discussion till now suggests just the opposite: The family is not made to close in on itself but to radiate outward toward a greater horizon. Let's put this even more forcefully: If the family refuses to go beyond its own boundaries, contenting itself instead with the pursuit of purely private goals, it ceases to be a true family.

This claim may sound overblown, but it follows logically from everything we've said so far about the roots of love from which the family grows. The spouses' capacity to love each other hinges on their covenant with the very Source from whom their love flows. This covenant incorporates them in its turn into the larger divine design and transforms them into collaborators with the Creator's plan to transmit life through the sequence of the generations. When a husband and wife take up the baton and share the gift of life in their turn, they assume a measure of responsibility, not just for their own children, but for the future of God's whole intergenerational project of communicating life to mankind.

The family is based on an expansive energy of love that by its very nature strives beyond the individual family members, or even the familial unit as a whole, to radiate actively at the heart of the world. The ripening of love we've traced in the previous chapters of the book hardwires a social mission into the very heart of the family. The family dynamic is essentially a social dynamic, and it's this outward thrust of familial life that we want to explore in this concluding reflection. What, then, is the family's role in the social order? This question is easy to formulate, yet the answer to which John Paul II's thought leads us utterly transforms our conventional understanding of man's coexistence in society.

Social Life and the Common Good

A basic premise of Catholic social teaching is that life together in society rests on what the theologians call the "common good."[1] But what is the actual substance of the common good? If we want to answer this question we have to answer another as well (because in the end the two questions are one): Why, exactly, is it good for people to live together in society in the first place?

One common account of why it's good for human beings to form societies is based on what we might call a "division of social labor." On this view, the reason it's good for (say) taxi drivers, bakers, and barbers to live in society is that each profession benefits the others by providing services that the others can't efficiently perform for themselves. This "tit for tat" approach, which essentially defines the common good as the sum of the practical advantages we gain by living with others, isn't completely false. Nevertheless, it ultimately fails to capture the whole truth about the common good. Remember that, in order to explain what holds society together, the question we have to answer is not What do we get out of one another? but What makes it worthwhile for us to participate in one another's lives at all?

Properly refocusing the question about the common good helps us perceive the flaw in the approach we've critiqued under the moniker of the "social division of labor." And the flaw is this: The division of labor theory overlooks the fact that common life itself is already a fundamental good in its own right. This theory forgets that participation in communities is itself a key ingredient of our humanity. Why is the neglect of this truth such a bad thing? Because if we lose sight of the fact that it's simply good for human persons to be together, even forgetting for the moment the practical benefits they might gain from their coexistence, then we no longer have any argument for defending the very bedrock upon which our civilization is built: the dignity of the human person. The division of social labor theory has eyes only for what we get out of each other; it inclines us to look at our fellow human beings only in terms of our own interests. By definition, such an approach is blind to the dignity of the human person, which is based on the principle that he or she is never to be used as a means to achieve my private goals and must never be stripped down to a mere function of my own private interests.

If we want to do justice to the dignity of the human person, we need a more generous vision of the common good; the common good needs to be based on a broader foundation than mere mutual self-interest. It's important to stress, though, that the more robust account of the common good we need doesn't rule out the (grateful) recognition of the benefits society brings us. Quite to the contrary, this fuller sense of the common good is the only approach that enables us properly to acknowledge these benefits in the first place. Unless our life in common were based on at least a vague inkling that to be with other persons is already a good in itself, nothing could stop society from degenerating into a violent struggle among private interests. In the latter scenario, the most we could hope for would be a bit of order imposed more or less brutally on the rising tide of chaos. Society would be like rush-hour traffic on a Friday afternoon; the only thing standing between a million motorists eager to get home for the weekend and total insanity would be . . . the police. An order maintained by force may be better than no order at all, but it falls woefully short of the bonds established by the recognition of the genuine common good; at best, it is a fragile truce always trembling on the verge of new conflict.

The metaphor of the functioning of a hydroelectric plant will illustrate the insufficiency of external constraints to hold society together. The plant engineers oversee the building of the dam and make sure the generators run smoothly. Nevertheless, their organizational labors would be futile without the primal force of the waterfall that actually turns the turbines. Analogously, political structures and legal codes are necessary for the common good, but the health of a society depends on a more original power. The primal energy turning the turbines of society is the experience that communal life with other persons is good for its own sake. We've purposely chosen the word "experience" to highlight that the person's perception of the common good isn't based simply on an idea. It rests on a firsthand acquaintance with the common good that is available to all human beings from the very first moments of their earthly journey. Enter the family.

THE COMMON GOOD OF THE SPOUSES

Our basic thesis is simple: The family is a school that introduces us experientially into the genuine common good on which alone a stable society can be built. Our exploration of this thesis begins with the marriage covenant between man and woman. What does their union teach them about the common good?

Our earlier discussion of original unity concluded that man and woman experience their encounter as a new creation. When he or she enters my life, my (prospective) spouse opens up new dimensions of my existence (and vice versa). The result is a new unity that makes each of us more truly him- or herself: "New people—Teresa and Andrew—two until now but still not one, one from now on though still two" (*JS*, 39). Marriage creates a communion of persons, which *is itself the common good of the spouses*:

> marital consent defines and consolidates *the good common to marriage* . . . "I, N., take you, N., to be my wife / husband. I promise to be true to you in good times and in bad, in sickness and in health. I will love you and honor you all the days of my life" . . . The words of consent define the common good of . . . the spouses: love, fidelity, honor, the permanence of their union until death—"all the days of my life" . . . The common good, by its very nature, both unites individual persons and ensures the true good of each. (John Paul II, *Letter to Families*, 10)

The common good of the matrimonial bond, it is important to see, is not inimical to the self-interest of the two partners. Rather, their communion is the foundation of all they are and have—and so of their very "selves" and "interests"—in the first place. It is good for the spouses to be together, not simply because each confers benefits on the other, but because each gives the other room to exist in the fullness of his or her humanity. The couple's togetherness itself is already a good. In fact, it is the greatest of their shared goods, insofar as it is the basis and foundation of any further good they may attain together. Once again, marriage does not suppress self-interest on the part of the spouses, but defines what it means for them to be "selves" in the first place.

Notice that the communion of love and life that is the common good of marriage does not rob the partners of their freedom. On the contrary, matrimony itself is the reconciliation of personal freedom with the common good; the partners' freedom is not threatened by the common good of the marital bond; their freedom is one and the same thing as their participation in it. By the same token, the marital relationship gives spouses a new "angle" on their life in society. The partners no longer say "my freedom ends where yours begins," but "my freedom starts where yours does, and we grow in freedom only through our togetherness."

Carlo Cardinal Caffarra illustrates this point with a helpful contrast between the common good and the Gross National Product. The GNP, remember, is the *sum* of individual wealth creation. A high GNP needn't mean that everyone is generating the same amount of wealth; it can also mean (and all too often does mean) that a few individuals produce "extra" wealth to compensate for the low economic output of their poorer neighbors. Clearly, the common good of the family isn't susceptible to this sort of calculation. As Cardinal Caffarra points out, the family's common good is less like a *sum* and more like a *product*. Thus, if one of the factors is zero, the total will be zero as well, no matter how much the other family members have. The suffering of one member affects the whole, nor can the flourishing of one offset the suffering of another. This suggests a new "formula" for "calculating" the familial common good: "The more *common* the good, the *more properly one's own* it will also be" (*Letter to Families*, 10).

THE COMMON GOOD OF THE CHILD

The spouses' participation in the common good of marriage comes to fulfillment with the conception and birth of the children who embody the fruit of their love. Let's try to define more precisely the new dimension of the common good that enters into play as the spousal *communion of persons* expands into the *community* of father, mother, and child (*Letter to Families*, 7).

Take the experience of an expectant mother. Her pregnancy is a "schooling" in the common good, for she learns in her own flesh that communion with her child is a good thing in itself—not because the child fills some function in her life, but because the child's very existence is a source of joy. Accordingly, one of the crucial tasks incumbent on women in society is to witness to the dignity of the person, a dignity that the sheer fact of their being women suits them to experience in a unique way:

> Motherhood involves a special communion with the mystery of life, as it develops in the woman's womb. The mother is filled with wonder at this mystery of life, and "understands" with unique intuition what is happening inside her ... This unique contact with the new human being developing within her gives rise to an attitude towards human beings—not only towards

her own child, but every human being—which profoundly marks the woman's personality. It is commonly thought that *women* are more capable than men of paying attention *to another person*, and that motherhood develops this predisposition even more. (*MD*, 18)

Of course, the child isn't the common good of the mother alone. The child is the common good of the whole couple, the fruit and the seal of their one-flesh communion. The child is a common good that demands to be valued by both parents for his or her own sake:

Is not every child a "particle" of that common good without which human communities break down and risk extinction? Could this ever really be denied? The child becomes a gift to its brothers, sisters, parents and entire family . . . Yes! *Man is a common good*: a common good of the family and of humanity, of individual groups and of different communities. (*Letter to Families*, 11)

John Paul II's words vividly capture the family's irreplaceable role as the "habitat" in which the very existence of the person—and not merely the benefits he provides others—is welcomed as a good that enriches everyone else. On the one hand, the child embodies for his parents the truth that each person, by his very existence, *is* a common good. On the other hand, the loving welcome the child receives from his parents brings home to the child himself that the dignity of the person is the essence of the common good. In other areas of society such as the workplace, we can never be entirely sure that our worth isn't being measured by our productivity. After all, we can always be "replaced" by another worker who will do more or less the same job. By contrast, the very nature of the family stands or falls with the irreplaceable and unique dignity of the person.

The family is called to be a "school" of experiential learning where children are initiated in a practical way into the substance of the common good. A healthy family teaches the child to live together with others in society—not simply by inculcating in him a few basic rules of behavior, but by infusing him with a concrete feeling for the dignity of the person that inclines him to see each human being as a common good. By bringing this indispensable lesson home to us, the family makes us agents of a truly humane social order.

THE SOURCE OF THE COMMON GOOD

The foregoing discussion has readied us for a new step in our argument: The family's mission isn't just to introduce us into the social dimension of the common good. The family is also called upon to initiate us into the ultimate horizon within which society lives and moves and has its being. Our next step is accordingly to consider how the family opens our eyes toward the ultimate Source of the common good.

Let's start with an issue that, at first sight, may seem unrelated to the family but is actually intimately bound up with it. We're all acutely conscious of, and anxious about, the specter of ecological catastrophe. We all know, too, that many people suppose that expanded regulation and new technology are sufficient to solve the problem. Unfortunately, this assumption is a potentially costly misconception, which overlooks the real root of our ecological imbalance: our collective delusion that man can arbitrarily reinvent the substance of the common good. "In his desire to have and to enjoy rather than to be and to grow," John Paul II diagnoses, "man consumes the resources of the earth and his own life in an excessive and disordered way."[2] If the pope's analysis of the roots of the ecological crisis is correct, then addressing the problem requires rethinking our relationship with nature. We need to recover a sense of the natural world, not simply as a set of resources to be exploited but as a home of communion in which we live out our destiny together.

We have only apparently strayed from the topic of the family. After all, the common good of the family is based on the acceptance of *natural* givens such as the language of masculinity and femininity (which the spouses don't create) and the fruitfulness that is written into the grammar of that language by the Creator himself. By the same logic, the family's mission is to foster our awareness of belonging to, and our proper reverence for, nature. This is why John Paul II speaks of the family as the first and fundamental "structure of human ecology" (*Centesimus Annus*, 39) that teaches us a more generous and humane sense of the common good.

The point we've just made about man's relationship with nature can be extended to his relationship with the culture in which he lives. Notice that culture is a way of weaving together past and future; culture is inseparable from the ongoing history of the people that embody it. Culture, we could say, is a legacy we receive from the past as a trust for the future generations whose lives will depend on the decisions we make here and now.[3] Since human nature has a cultural profile as well, we can't do justice to the common good of a society if we lose sight of the broader horizon of the whole human family or fail in reverence for the patrimony we have received from our ancestors and are called to pass on to our children in turn.

Culture, we could say, is the work of incorporating our own historical moment into the great tapestry of life in which past, present, and future are inextricably interwoven. It should be immediately obvious that the family is eminently suited to carry out this work of integration. On the one hand, the family is the transmitter of a heritage that children are called on to receive with gratitude from their parents and grandparents and to pass on to their own posterity in their turn. Family life also teaches parents to regard the good of their children as their own good, and thus disposes them to a vigorous concern for society's future. The heritage of the past equips man for the future, weaving him into the unbroken intergenerational thread of the human story. The family transforms "conjugal communion [into] a communion of generations" (*Letter to Families*, 10).

We could sum up what we've seen so far in a simple statement: The family is the basic context in which we human beings receive both nature and culture as a gift entrusted to our stewardship. This thesis suggests the corollary that, unless we are saturated by the awareness that reality is a gift committed to our loving and grateful care, we cannot expect to build up the common good. Another way of putting this is that "duties" come before "rights." Stefano Fontana, who directs Cardinal Van Thuân's International Observatory for the Social Doctrine of the Church, argues that "we really have to go back to the priority of duty . . . We do not produce ourselves, but receive . . . ourselves. We do not produce nature, but receive . . . it. We do not produce culture, but receive . . . it. Of course, we do also produce, but our production is based on an original receiving."[4] Clearly, the family is eminently suited to foster the respect for the priority of duty Fontana calls for, because the family is a tissue of duties of love woven in response to the primordial gift of life and of the original love at its origin.

Ultimately, the heritage of nature and culture invites us to seek the fundamental origin of these gifts. Society cannot evade the question of the Source of the common good. Admittedly, an influential strand of modern thought has argued that believers and nonbelievers can live in common only if they shape public life according to rules that are detached from the acknowledgment of the presence of God. A few days before his election to the papacy, Benedict XVI criticized this exclusion of God from public life.[5] The then Cardinal Ratzinger pointed to the history of the twentieth century, which, he argued, demonstrates with all desirable clarity that attempts to construct society "as if God did not exist" lead inevitably to the eclipse of human dignity. Ratzinger was not downplaying the real questions raised by the fact of pluralism. He was merely arguing that the common good (without which there can be no society in the first place) can endure only if we act "as if God *did* exist." By the same logic, Ratzinger reasoned, rejection of God from the public realm ultimately undermines any common awareness of the good or the dignity of man.[6]

Ratzinger's reflections on God and public life bring us back to the family, which is man's first introduction to the original Source of goodness, the common Father from whom "every family is named" (see Eph. 3:14–15). If this is right, then family life, by opening us to God, also orients us to the ultimate horizon that makes common life in society possible. In the next section we'll explore in greater depth the family's mission as the source and blueprint of the common good, a mission that undergirds the family's role as the basic cell of community.

FAMILY, BECOME WHAT YOU ARE!

The family circle is man's first and foundational exposure to the common good of society: Such is the preliminary conclusion we've reached so far in our discussion. But we still have to consider how the family is supposed to live out its mission in society. What, precisely, is the family supposed to *do*? A bit of reflection suffices to show that the answer to this question doesn't lie in some tightly circumscribed activity or activities lying outside of family life itself. After all, society as a whole is generated from the family—not only physically through the birth of new members, but also spiritually through the education of the whole person in love. But if the family is the birthplace of society in its entirety, its essential social task can't be some extra function outside of itself. The family's job in society consists simply in becoming what it already is: the matrix of the common good.

The notion of "social capital" provides a handy way to illustrate the family's basic role in society. Social capital, the economists tell us, is a set of virtues—such as trust, friendship, openness to others, and the like—that hold society together. This definition of social capital fits our account of the family to a tee. Stable, fruitful marriage between man and woman is the primary source of social capital, a source that no other arrangement can replace but can only benefit from parasitically. Accordingly, the state has a natural duty to protect and foster the family. Indeed, the state is called upon to favor the family based upon marriage over other forms of "weak love," such as cohabitation, because the family is an irreplaceable school of the common good that is the basis of all social life in the first place.

When the state no longer fosters the connection between the

family and the common good, the most we can hope for is an attempt to suppress or delay the "war of all against all" that eventually leads to the collapse of civilization. This consideration lends special urgency to the following statement from the *Compendium of the Social Doctrine of the Church*: "[T]he priority of the family over society and over the State must be affirmed... The family, then, does not exist for society or the State, but society and the State exist for the family."[7]

The family generates the person as a social being whose experiential understanding of the common good equips him to promote and serve a truly humane social order. Catholic social teaching packs this insight into a simple formula. The family, this teaching tells us, is the first cell of society. The word "cell" implies much more than the idea that the family is the basic building block of society. For whereas one building block (such as a brick) can be exchanged for another without affecting the structure of the building, the family—like the cell of a body—contains the genetic blueprint of the whole social edifice. Just as each cell contains the DNA of the entire body, the family contains the whole idea of the common good, because the family is the natural "habitat" into which the dignity of the person is born.

The famous Bernini colonnade that encloses Saint Peter's Square in Rome provides a helpful illustration of the point we're making here. As is well known, the colonnade has an elliptical shape. This means that you have to stand at one of the focal points of the ellipse to glimpse the harmony of the whole structure. It's only from this privileged point of view, in other words, that you can perceive the unity of the whole design. Now suppose you were an architect commissioned to add to Bernini's masterpiece without violating the harmony of his original conception. Your plans for the addition would have to ensure that anyone surveying the colonnade from one of its focal points would still perceive the harmony of Bernini's original idea.

The family is like the focal point of the ellipse in Bernini's colonnade, the privileged vantage point from which to perceive the unity of society in its overall design. The family alone, of course, cannot provide all the materials needed for the construction of society. Nevertheless, the family furnishes something even more important: the home and reference point of social unity, the irreplaceable experience from which any work for the common good derives its basic pattern and purpose.

Jesus said to the disciples: "You are the light of the world" (Matt. 5:14). The Lord's words apply in a special way to the family. Light, after all, fulfills its "mission" of bestowing warmth and visibility not by some extra activity added to its nature, but simply by being what it is. Similarly, just as the mission of the sun is nothing other than to shine, the mission of the family is just to be itself. John Paul II was calling the family to this essential mission when he exclaimed: "Family, become what you are!" What happens when the family becomes what it is? Here is John Paul II's answer:

> Since in God's plan it has been established as an "intimate community of life and love," the family has the mission to become more and more what it is, that is to say, a community of life and love . . . [T]he essence and role of the family are in the final analysis specified by love. Hence the family has the mission to guard, reveal and communicate love, and this is a living reflection of and a real sharing in God's love for humanity and the love of Christ the Lord for the Church His bride. (*Familiaris Consortio*, 17)

If we want a civilization of love, then we must foster the family, since the family is the generative matrix from which society is born. John Paul has written: *"Through the family passes the primary current of the civilization of love,"* which thus "finds therein its 'social foundations' " (*Letter to Families*, 15). The pope does not mean to reduce the family to a mere means for constructing the civilization of love. On the contrary, his point is that the civilization of love is nothing but the accumulated light radiating from the family, while the family itself is "the center and the heart of the civilization of love" (*Letter to Families*, 13).

THE MISSION OF THE FAMILY THE MISSION OF THE CHURCH

Let's review the ground we've covered so far: The experience of love in the family, we've said, is the source of society, the DNA-like embodiment of its overall pattern and purpose, which governs and guides the building of a civilization of love. This allusion to the civilization of love brings us a step further in the argument, for it reminds us that the family is a church in miniature, a "domestic church," just as the Church is a family writ large. To illustrate the reciprocal relation between the Church and the family, Pope Benedict uses the example of Prisca and Aquila, a Christian couple mentioned in the Epistles of Saint Paul who offered their home for the celebration of the Eucharist:

In the house of Aquila and Prisca, therefore, the Church gathered, the convocation of Christ, which celebrates here the Sacred Mysteries . . . [E]very home can transform itself into a little church . . . Not by chance does Paul compare, in the Letter to the Ephesians, the matrimonial relationship to the spousal communion that happens between Christ and the Church [cf. Eph. 5:25–33]. Even more, we can maintain that the Apostle indirectly models the life of the entire Church on that of the family. And the Church, in reality, is the family of God.[8]

We have described the family's mission of enabling the experience of love that is the root of the common good. The family, we said, is the hearth from which the light of love spreads out to vivify the structures of society. Or, varying the metaphor, the family is the focal point from which we perceive the unity of the whole structure of society. Significantly, the mission of the Church can be described in similar terms. The Church exists, after all, to radiate God's love into the world. The Church is the sacrament of love that both shows forth and effects man's union with God and man's union with man (see *LG*, 1).

The love the Church embodies for the world is not some abstract benevolence or tolerance. Rather, the love the Church manifests has a face: the face of the Son and Bridegroom who laid down his life for his Bride. Since Jesus Christ is the Bridegroom, the love that the Church reveals is as concrete as the love between husband and wife. Even more, the communion between the Bridegroom and his Bride is the mirror in which the family glimpses the truth about itself and its mission. The Church is the natural habitat of the family, where the truth of familial love is revealed, purified, and emboldened to live out its vocation.

The Church assists the family in its task of building a home for love and schooling the heart to perceive the dignity of the human being. At the same time, the family's accomplishment of this task enables the Church to be present in society. Although the Church's duty is not to take over the functions of the state, it *does* play a crucial role in public life all the same. Christianity is by its very essence a public religion that is called to transform the world by giving it the shape of the love that is sacramentally embodied in the Church. As we've just suggested, the Church carries out this mission of transformation precisely by spreading the light of the Gospel to and through the family. Since the family is the school of the common good where man learns how to build the civilization of love, the Church's presence in the family not only illumines the lives of the individuals who compose it, but also shines through them to guide the task of achieving the fullness of the common good. Conversely, if the Gospel does not enliven the family, strengthening the bond between husband and wife, parents and children, brothers and sisters, Christianity becomes bloodless and loses its purchase on society. Which, of course, only reinforces our main point: *The Church radiates the form of Christian love to the whole of society through the family, which is the way of the Church* (see *Letter to Families,* 2).

The image of Saint Peter's Square that we presented just now suggests a fitting conclusion to our reflections. The focal points of Bernini's ellipse-shaped colonnade, we said, illustrate the family's vocation to embody the pattern of a humane society. Significantly, Bernini compared the arms of his colonnade to those that the Church throws open to embrace the whole world. Bernini's image thus underscores the connection between the mission of the family and the mission of the Church. The Church is a circle of universal communion that embraces all people, but the center of the circle includes a special space for the family, a space opened up by Christ, the Son and the Bridegroom. When the family enters this space, it becomes what it is, a "domestic Church" that sheds the light of the Gospel—the light of communion—on the vocation and destiny of man and thus guides his work of building up the civilization of love.

NOTES

LIST OF ABBREVIATIONS: *ANF: Ante-Nicene Fathers.* CCL: Corpus Christianorum Latinorum. *GS: Gaudium et Spes. LG: Lumen Gentium. MD: Mulieris Dignitatem (Letter to Women). NPNF: A Select Library of Nicene and Post-Nicene Fathers of the Christian Church.* PG: Patrologial cursus completus. Accurante Jacques-Paul Migne. Series Graeca (Paris). PL: Patrologial cursus completus. Accurante Jacques-Paul Migne. Series Latina (Paris). *TOB: Man and Women He Created Them: A Theology of the Body.*

INTRODUCTION

1. John Paul II develops this thought in the first pages of *The Acting Person.* Man's experience of the world spills over into his experience of himself.

2. Saint Augustine, *Confessions* IV, iv, 9.

3. See *TOB*, 138.

4. Georges Bernanos, *The Diary of a Country Priest*, trans. Pamela Morris (New York: Carroll and Graf, 1983), 138.

CHAPTER I

1. On this topic, see Livio Melina, *Per una cultura della famiglia: Il linguaggio dell'amore* (Venezia: Marcianum Press, 2006).

2. T. S. Eliot, "The Dry Salvages," in *The Complete Poems and Plays, 1909–1950* (New York: Harcourt, Brace, 1952), 133.

3. See J. R. R. Tolkien, *The Silmarillion* (Boston: Houghton Mifflin, 2004).

4. See Gabriel Marcel, *The Mystery of Being*. vol. 1, *Reflection and Mystery*, trans. Rene Haque (South Bend, Ind.: St. Augustine's Press, 2001), 91: "[W]e are all tending to become bureaucrats, and not only in our outward behavior, but in our relations with ourselves. This is as much as to say that between ourselves and existence we are interposing thicker and thicker screens."

5. John Paul II, *Memory and Identity: Conversations at the Dawn of a Millennium* (New York: Rizzoli, 2005), 151.

6. Saint Augustine, *Confessions* I, 1 (Chadwick, p. 3).

7. See *TOB*, 152.

8. See Karol Wojtyla, "The Place Within," in *Collected Poems*, 116.

9. See Gabriel Marcel, *The Mystery of Being*, 90. Marcel compares the experience of being in the body to a "small child who comes up to us with shining eyes, who seems to be saying: 'Here I am! What luck!' " My being is a manifest being, there is a radiance of being at once toward myself and toward others.

10. See Maurice Merleau-Ponty, *Phenomenology of Perception* (London and New York: Routledge, 2003), 174: "The body is to be compared, not to a physical object, but rather to a work of art."

11. Saint Augustine, *Confessions* I, 1: "*fecisti nos ad te*."

12. John Paul II, Encyclical *Laborem Exercens* (On Human Work), 6.

13. See Saint Symeon the New Theologian, *Hymns* II, vv. 19–27 (*Sources Chrétiennes* 156, 178–79). (The text is quoted by John Paul II in his Apostolic Exhortation *Vita Consecrata*, 20.)

CHAPTER 2

1. See *TOB*, 161: "The definitive creation of man consists in the creation of the unity of two beings." Eve was created *"in order that the solitary 'man' may by God's creative initiative reemerge from that moment* in his double unity as male and female" (*TOB*, 159).

2. See Josef Pieper, *Faith, Hope, Love* (San Francisco: Ignatius Press, 1997), 163–86.

3. "It is here in Genesis 2:23 that we come across the distinction between *ish* and *issah* for the first time" (*TOB*, 159).

4. Ovid, *Metamorphoses*, III, 433–38, trans. A. Mahoney (New York: Calvin Blanchard, 1855).

5. See Angelo Scola, *Uomo-Donna. Il "caso serio" dell'amore* (Genova and Milano: Marietti, 2002), 21.

6. José Granados, "The Unity of the Human Person Under the Light of Love" in *The Way of Love: Reflections on Pope Benedict XVI's Encyclical Deus Caritas Est*, edited by Carl A. Anderson and Livio Melina (San Francisco: Ignatius Press, 2006), 91–106.

7. Saint Augustine, *Confessions* XIII, ix, 10 (Chadwick, p. 278).

8. See *LR*, 199: "Sentiment may, however, play an important auxiliary role in the whole process of sublimation. For the value of the person must be not merely understood by the cold light of reason but felt."

9. See Saint Augustine, *Enarrationes in Psalmos* 94, 2 (PL 37, 1217).

CHAPTER 3

1. The then Cardinal Ratzinger comments on this story in Joseph Ratzinger, *God and the World: A Conversation with Peter Seewald* (San Francisco: Ignatius Press, 2002), 195: "I think that is such a lovely little incident, in which you can see that sometimes a rose, a little act of giving, of affection, of acceptance of the other person, can be more than many coins or other material gifts."

2. See *Adversus Haereses*, book IV, chapter 18, no. 1 (*Sources Chrétiennes*, vol. 100, p. 596) (*ANF* 484).

3. Ralph Waldo Emerson, "Essay V," in *Essays* (London: Dent, 1906), 291; quoted in Kenneth L. Schmitz, *The Gift: Creation* (Milwaukee: Marquette University Press, 1982), 59.

4. *The Spiritual Exercises of St. Ignatius, Based on Studies in the Language of the Autograph*, trans. Louis J. Puhd (Chicago: Loyola Press, 1951), 101.

5. Saint John of the Cross, "Letter 26 to M. M. de la Encarnación, July 6, 1591" in *The Collected Works of Saint John of the Cross*, trans. Kieran Kavanaugh and Otilio Rodriguez (Washington, DC: Institute of Carmelite Studies Publications, 1991).

6. See Elizabeth Barrett Browning, *Sonnets from the Portuguese*, number XIV, in *The Complete Poetical Works of Elizabeth Barrett Browning* (Whitefish, MT: Kessinger Publishing, 2005), 421.

7. Oral presentation given at the John Paul II Institute for Studies on Marriage and Family, Rome, April 27, 2006.

8. Saint Irenaeus of Lyons, *Adversus haereses*, book IV, chapter 14, no. 1 (*Sources Chrétiennes*, vol. 100, p. 538).

9. In the words of Saint Augustine: "People are moved to wonder by mountain peaks, by vast waves of the sea, by broad waterfalls on rivers, by the all-embracing extent of the ocean, by the revolutions of the stars. But in themselves they are uninterested" (*Confessions* X, viii, 15 [Chadwick, p. 187]).

10. Thornton Wilder, *Our Town: A Play in Three Acts* (London: Samuel French, 1965), 83.

11. John Paul writes: "This finding of oneself in one's own gift becomes the source of a new gift of self that grows by the power of the inner disposition of the exchange of the gift and in the measure in which it encounters the same and even deeper acceptance and welcome as the fruit of an ever more intense consciousness of the gift itself" (*TOB*, 197).

12. See Jean Guitton, *Human Love* (Chicago: Franciscan Herald Press, 1966), 82.

13. Dante Alighieri, *Purgatorio* VII, 40–60.

14. See also *TOB*, 157.

CHAPTER 4

1. See *Dominum et Vivificantem*, 34: "This means not only rationality and freedom as constitutive properties of human nature, but also, from the very beginning, the capacity of having a personal relationship with God, as 'I' and 'you,' and therefore the capacity of having a covenant, which will take place in God's salvific communication with man."

2. See Saint Athanasius, *De Incarnatione Verbi* 1, 3. English translation: *St. Athanasius on the Incarnation: The Treatise De incarnatione Verbi Dei*, trans. Penelope Lawson (Crestwood, NY: St. Vladimir's Seminary Press, 1982), 28.

3. See *Ambiguum 7*, PG, vol. 91, col. 1084 A; see also Saint Cyril of Alexandria: "For it is the quality of our comportment that makes us similar to God, and it is the exercise of the virtues that imprints on us the features of the divine image" (PG, vol. 75, col. 673BC), quoted in Christoph Schönborn, *God's Human Face: The Christ-Icon* (San Francisco: Ignatius Press, 1994), 100.

4. See *MD*, 7.

5. Address of His Holiness Benedict XVI to the Participants in the Ecclesial Diocesan Convention of Rome, June 6, 2005.

6. See *Letter to Families*, 9. This explains what Vatican II means when it teaches that the image of God includes the social dimension of the person (*GS*, 12).

7. On this topic, see Livio Melina, *Per una cultura della famiglia: Il linguaggio dell'amore* (Venezia: Marcianum Press, 2006), 14–29.

8. "In this first expression of the man, 'flesh from my flesh' contains also a reference to that by which that body is authentically human and thus to that which determines man as a person, that is, as a being that is, also in all its bodiliness, 'similar' to God" (*TOB*, 164).

9. See Tertullian, *On the Resurrection of the Flesh*, chap. 9, no. 1 in *De resurrectione carnis liber. Treatise on the Resurrection*, trans. Ernest Evans (London: Society for Promoting Christian Knowledge, 1960), 27.

10. John Paul II calls the Spirit the "Person-Gift" in his encyclical *Dominum et Vivificantem* 10, 22–23.

11. Saint Seraphim of Sarov, *Spiritual Instructions*, 110–11, quoted by Marko Ivan Rupnik, *In the Fire of the Burning Bush: An Initiation to the Spiritual Life* (Grand Rapids, Mich.: Eerdmans, 2004), 30.

12. See Saint Augustine, *De Trinitate*, Book XV, chap. VI, no. 10 (CCL, vol. 50, p. 472).

CHAPTER 5

1. Saint Augustine, *Confessions*, XIII, ix, 10 (Chadwick, p. 278).

2. For this interpretation, see Bruna Costacurta, "Exegesis: Reading the Scriptures in Faith," in José Granados, Carlos Granados, and Luis Sánchez-Navarro, eds., *Opening Up the Scriptures: Joseph Ratzinger and the Foundations of Scriptural Interpretation* (Grand Rapids, Mich.: Eerdmans, 2008), 79–86.

3. "The original acceptance of the body was in some sense the basis of the acceptance of the whole visible world. And in its turn, it was for man the guarantee of his rule over the world, over the earth, which he was to subdue" (*TOB*, 241).

4. Karol Wojtyla, *Collected Poems*, 115.

5. Saint Augustine, *Confessions*, VIII, x, 22 (Chadwick, p. 148).

6. Saint Augustine, *Confessions*, VI, xvi, 26 (Chadwick, p. 110).

7. See Dante Alighieri, *Inferno*, V, 103–5 (Esolen, p. 51).

8. See Dante Alighieri, *Inferno*, V, 43 (Esolen, p. 47).

9. See *LR*, 172: "Humility is the proper attitude towards all true greatness, including one's own greatness as a human being, but above all towards the greatness which is not oneself, which is beyond one's self. The human body must be 'humble' in face of the greatness represented by the person: for in the person resides the true and definitive greatness of man. Furthermore, the human body must 'humble itself' in face of the magnitude represented by love.... 'The body' must also show humility in the face of human happiness."

CHAPTER 6

1. John Paul II illustrates this point drawing on the biblical book of the Song of Songs; cf. *TOB*, 586: "The language of the body that runs through the verses of the Song of Songs seems to have its limits. Love shows itself as greater than what the 'body' is able to express. And it is at this point that its weakness becomes in some way a 'language of the body.' 'I am sick with love,' says the bride, as if she wanted to bear witness to the fragility of the subject that bears the love of both."

2. *Capitum de caritate*, Book IV, chap. 100 (PG 90, 1073 A).

3. *TOB*, 221.

4. The Letter to the Hebrews gives witness to what we just said: Christ's body is prepared by the Father, who forms it in his mother's womb (see Jer. 1:5). In fact, upon entering into the world, the Son says: "A body hast thou prepared for me. . . . Lo, I have come to do thy will" (Heb. 10:5–7). The connection of these two sentences is important: The words in which the Son declares his Sonship in obedience to the Father—"behold, I come to do your will"—fully reveal the true dignity of the body—"a body you prepared for me."

5. Saint Leo the Great, *Sermon XXI*, 3 (*Sources Chrétiennes*, vol. 22a, p. 72).

6. See *Salvifici Doloris*, 9.

7. Fyodor Dostoyevsky, *The Brothers Karamazov: A Novel in Four Parts with Epilogue*, trans. Richard Pevear and Larissa Volokhonsky (New York: Farrar, Straus and Giroux, 2002), 74.

8. Dostoyevsky, *The Brothers Karamazov*, 285.

9. See José Granados, "Toward a Theology of the Suffering Body," in *Communio: International Catholic Review* 33 (2006), 540–63.

10. Saint Irenaeus of Lyons, *Adversus Haereses*, Book III, chap. 24, no. 1 (*Sources Chrétiennes*, vol. 211, p. 472) (*ANF* 458).

11. Letter to Smyrna 1, in *The Epistles of St. Clement of Rome and St. Ignatius of Antioch*, trans. James A. Kleist (Mahwah, NJ: Paulist Press: 1946), 90.

CHAPTER 7

1. See Karol Wojtyla, *Collected Plays*, 392–93.

2. Dante Alighieri, *Paradiso* I, 135–41 (Esolen, p. 11).

3. Saint Augustine, *Confessions*, XIII, IX, 10 (Chadwick, p. 278).

4. John Paul II insists that man must learn "what the meaning of the body is . . . in the sphere of the interior reactions of his own heart" (*TOB*, 320). Christ calls the inner man to a more mature discernment of the various movements of his own heart.

5. See Saint Gregory of Nazianzus, *Oratio* XLIII, 20 (PG 36, 521). English translation: *NPNF* 7, p. 402, slightly modified.

6. See Saint Augustine, *De Moribus Ecclesiae Catholicae* I, 15, 25. English translation: *NPNF* 4 (1887), p. 48.

7. Saint Augustine, *Confessions* X, xxix, 40 (Chadwick, p. 202).

8. Saint Augustine, *De Moribus Ecclesiae Catholicae* I, 15, 25. English translation: *NPNF* 4 (1887), p. 48.

9. See Søren Kierkegaard, *Purity of Heart Is to Will One Thing*, trans. Douglas Van Steere (New York: Harper & Row, 1956).

10. Dante Alighieri, *Purgatorio* XXVII, 132–42 (Esolen, p. 297).

11. Saint Augustine, *Confessions* XIII, ix, 10 (Chadwick, p. 278).

12. Piety, "which springs from the profound consciousness of the mystery of Christ, must constitute the basis of the reciprocal relations between the spouses" (*TOB*, 472).

13. Dante Alighieri, *Purgatorio* X, 41–45 (Esolen, p. 107):

> for the one who opened Heaven's high love
> was there in image, she who turned the key,
> and in her pose was stamped the spoken word,
> exactly as a seal in molten wax:
> *Behold, I am the handmaid of the Lord.*

CHAPTER 8

1. See Tertullian, *Ad Uxorem*, Book II, paragraph VIII, 6–8: CCL, I, 393. The text is quoted in *Familiaris Consortio*, 13, from which we take the translation cited here.

2. George Bernard Shaw, *Getting Married*, in *The Doctor's Dilemma, Getting Married and the Shewing-Up of Blanco Posnet* (New York: Brentano's, 1915), 139.

3. Address of His Holiness Benedict XVI to the Participants in the Ecclesial Diocesan Convention of Rome, June 6, 2005.

4. "Even in the begetting of children marriage reflects its divine model, God's love for man. In man and woman, fatherhood and motherhood, like the body and like love, cannot be limited to the biological: life is entirely given only when, by birth, love and meaning are also given, which make it possible to say yes to this life" (Address of His Holiness Benedict XVI to the Participants in the Ecclesial Diocesan Convention of Rome, June 6, 2005).

5. The painting is called *First Steps*, and Van Gogh modeled it on a work by Jean-François Millet.

6. Benedict XVI, Message addressed to Mons. Livio Melina, President of the John Paul II Pontifical Institute for Studies on Marriage and Family, on the Occasion of the 40th Anniversary of Paul VI's Encyclical *Humanae Vitae*, October 2, 2008.

7. Benedict XVI, Message addressed to Mons. Livio Melina, President of the John Paul II Pontifical Institute for Studies on Marriage and Family, on the Occasion of the 40th Anniversary of Paul VI's Encyclical *Humanae Vitae*, October 2, 2008.

8. See *Familiaris Consortio*, 32.

9. Sigrid Undset, *Kristin Lavransdatter*, trans. Tiina Nunnally (New York: Penguin, 2005), 1122.

CHAPTER 9

1. See Gabriel Marcel, *The Mystery of Being*, vol. 2, *Faith and Reality*, trans. G. S. Fraser (South Bend, Ind.: St. Augustine's Press, 2001), 153.

2. See Tertullian, *De resurrectione carnis*, 36. English translation: Tertullian, *De resurrectione carnis liber. Treatise on the Resurrection*, trans. Ernest Evans (London: Society for Promoting Christian Knowledge, 1960), 101 (translation slightly modified).

3. "Spiritualization signifies not only that the spirit will master the body, but, I would say, that it will also fully permeate the body and the powers of the spirit will permeate the energies of the body" (*TOB*, 391). "Nevertheless, this should not be understood as a definitive 'victory' of the spirit over the body. The resurrection will consist in the perfect participation of all that is bodily in man in all that is spiritual in him. At the same time, it will consist in the perfect realization of what is personal in man" (*TOB*, 392).

4. Pseudo-Macarius, Fifteenth Homily, 38 (PG, vol. 34, col. 602).

5. See Dante Alighieri, *Purgatorio* XV, 67–75 (Esolen, p. 163).

6. Saint Methodius, *Symposium* 1, 4 (English translation: Methodius of Olympus, *The Symposium: A Treatise on Chastity*). Trans. by H. Musurillo (New York: Paulist Press, 1958).

7. Maximus Confessor, *Gnostic Centuries* II, 28 (PG, vol. 90, col. 1092).

8. Saint Ignatius of Antioch, *Letter to Polycarp*, 5. English translation: Bart D. Ehrman, *The Apostolic Fathers*, Loeb Classical Library (Cambridge, Mass.: Harvard University Press, 2003), vol. 1, 315.

9. Saint Augustine, *Confessions* VIII, xi, 27 (Chadwick, p. 151).

10. See Paul Claudel, *The Tidings Brought to Mary: A Mystery*, trans. Louise Morgan Sill (London: Chatto & Windus, 1916), p. 122.

11. *Paradiso*, Canto XXXIII, 7 (Esolen, p. 351).

CHAPTER 10

1. The following reflections regarding the common good are indebted to Carlo Cardinal Caffarra, *"Famiglia e bene comune. Prolusione per*

l'Inaugurazione dell'Anno Accademico 2006/2007 del Pontificio Istituto Giovanni Paolo II per Studi su Matrimonio e Famiglia nel XXVI dalla Fondazione" (Vatican City, 2006).

2. See *Centesimus Annus*, 37: "In his desire to have and to enjoy rather than to be and to grow, man consumes the resources of the earth and his own life in an excessive and disordered way."

3. For further discussion of this point, see philosopher Hans Jonas's important book, *The Imperative of Responsibility: In Search of an Ethics for the Technological Age* (Chicago: University of Chicago Press, 1984).

4. See Stefano Fontana, *Per una politica dei doveri dopo il fallimento della stagione dei diritti* [For a politics of duties after the failure of the season of rights] (Siena: Cantagalli, 2006).

5. See Benedict XVI, *Christianity and the Crisis of Cultures* (San Francisco: Ignatius Press, 2006), 50–51.

6. The reason that this is the case should be clear from our discussion in earlier chapters of this book: Man's dignity is based on his nature as *imago Dei* (*GS*, 24).

7. Pontifical Council for Justice and Peace, *Compendium of the Social Doctrine of the Church* (Città del Vaticano and Washington, DC: Libreria Editrice Vaticana, 2005), 97.

8. "Priscilla and Aquila. General Audience of February 7, 2007," in Benedict XVI, *Jesus, the Apostles, and the Early Church: General Audiences 15 March 2006–14 February 2007* (San Francisco: Ignatius Press, 2007), 147–49.

BIBLIOGRAPHY

Anderson, Carl A. *A Civilization of Love: What Every Catholic Can Do to Transform the World*. New York: HarperOne, 2008.

Anderson, Carl A., and Livio Melina. *The Way of Love: Reflections on Pope Benedict XVI's Encyclical* Deus Caritas Est. San Francisco: Ignatius Press, 2006.

Benedict XVI. *God Is Love:* Deus Caritas Est. San Francisco: Ignatius Press, 2006.

Benedict XVI. *Saved in Hope:* Spe Salvi. San Francisco: Ignatius Press, 2008.

García de Haro, Ramón. *Marriage and the Family in the Documents of the Magisterium: A Course in the Theology of Marriage*. San Francisco: Ignatius Press, 1993.

Granados, José. *Mundat Caro, Regnat Caro: Il corpo, cardine della storia della salvezza*. Siena: Cantagalli, 2009.

———. "Toward a Theology of the Suffering Body." *Communio. International Catholic Review* 33 (2006): 540–63.

Guitton, Jean. *Human Love*. Chicago: Franciscan Herald Press, 1966.

Hildebrand, Dietrich von. *Purity: The Mystery of Christian Sexuality*. Steubenville, OH: Franciscan University Press, 1989.

John Paul II. *Letter to Families*. Washington, DC: United States Catholic Conference, 1994.

————. *Man and Woman He Created Them: A Theology of the Body*. Translated by Michael Waldstein. Boston: Pauline Books & Media, 2006.

————. *On the Dignity and Vocation of Women: Apostolic Letter* Mulieris Dignitatem. Washington, DC: United States Catholic Conference, 1988.

————. *On the Family: Apostolic Exhortation* Familiaris Consortio. Washington, DC: United States Catholic Conference, 1982.

————. *Redeemer of Man: Encyclical Letter* Redemptor Hominis. Washington, DC: United States Catholic Conference, 1979.

————. *Roman Triptych. Meditations*. Translated by Jerzy Peterkiewicz. Washington, DC: USCCB Publishing, 2003.

————. *The Splendor of Truth: Encyclical Letter* Veritatis Splendor. Washington, DC: United States Catholic Conference, 1993.

Kupczak, Jarosla. *Destined for Liberty: The Human Person in the Philosophy of Karol Wojtyla/John Paul II*. Washington, DC: CUA Press, 2000.

Marcel, Gabriel. *The Mystery of Being. I: Reflection and Mystery*. South Bend, IN: St. Augustine's Press, 2001.

Melina, Livio. *Per una cultura della famiglia: Il linguaggio dell'amore*. Venezia: Marcianum Press, 2006.

————. *Sharing in Christ's Virtues: For a Renewal of Moral Theology in Light of* Veritatis Splendor. Washington, DC: Catholic University of American Press, 2001.

Merleau-Ponty, Maurice. *Phenomenology of Perception*. London and New York: Routledge, 2003.

Noriega, José. *El destino del eros. Perspectivas de moral sexual*. Ediciones Palabra: Madrid, 2005.

Ouellet, Marc. *Divine Likeness: Toward a Trinitarian Anthropology of the Family*. Grand Rapids, MI: W. B. Eerdmans, 2006.

Pieper, Josef. *Faith, Hope, Love*. San Francisco: Ignatius Press, 1997.

Pontifical Council for Justice and Peace. *Compendium of the Social Doctrine of the Church*. Città del Vaticano and Washington, DC: Libreria Editrice Vaticana and (U.S.) Conference of Catholic Bishops, 2005.

Prokes, Mary Timothy. *Toward a Theology of the Body*. Grand Rapids, MI: W. B. Eerdmans, 1996.

Ratzinger, Joseph. *Daughter Zion*. San Francisco: Ignatius Press, 1983.

———. *To Look on Christ: Exercises in Faith, Hope, and Love*. New York, Crossroad Publishing Co., 1991.

Schindler, David L. *Heart of the World, Center of the Church: Communio Ecclesiology, Liberalism, and Liberation*. Grand Rapids, MI: W. B. Eerdmans, 1996.

———. "The significance of World and Culture for Moral Theology: *Veritatis Splendor* and the 'Nuptial-Sacramental' Nature of the Body." *Communio. International Catholic Review* 31 (2004): 111–42.

Schmitz, Kenneth L. *At the Center of the Human Drama: The Philosophical Anthropology of Karol Wojtyla/John Paul II*. Washington, DC: CUA Press, 1993.

———. *The Gift: Creation*. Milwaukee, WI: Marquette University Press, 1982.

Scola, Angelo. *The Nuptial Mystery*. Grand Rapids, MI: W. B. Eerdmans, 2005.

Shivanandan, Mary. *Crossing the Threshold of Love: A New Vision of Marriage in the Light of John Paul II's Anthropology.* Washington, DC: Catholic University of American Press, 1999.

Wojtyla, Karol. *The Acting Person.* Translated by Anna-Teresa Tymieniecka, *Analecta Husserliana.* Dordrecht, Boston: D. Reidel Publishing Company, 1979.

———. *The Collected Plays and Writings on Theater.* Berkeley: University of California Press, 1987.

———. *Collected Poems.* Translated by Jerzy Peterkiewicz. New York: Random House, 1982.

———. *The Jeweler's Shop: A Meditation on the Sacrament of Matrimony Passing on Occasion into a Drama.* San Francisco: Ignatius Press, 1992.

———. *Love and Responsibility.* San Francisco: Ignatius Press, 1993.